Catholic Bible Study

Ezekiel, Hebrews, Revelation

by

Father Andreas Hoeck, S.S.D.

and

Laurie Watson Manhardt, Ph.D.

EMMAUS
ROAD
PUBLISHING

Steubenville, Ohio
A Division of Catholics United for the Faith
www.emmausroad.org

Emmaus Road Publishing
827 North Fourth Street
Steubenville, OH 43952

Library of Congress Control Number: 2010929571
ISBN: 9781931018654

Cover design and layout by
Jacinta Calcut, Image Graphics & Design www.image-gd.com

Cover artwork:
Jan van Eyck (1395–1441 AD), *The Adoration of the Lamb*
Altarpiece—Cathedral of Saint Bavo, Ghent, Belgium

Nihil obstat: William Beckman, *Censor Deputatus*
Imprimatur: Most Reverend Charles Chaput, O.F.M.Cap., Archbishop of Denver
April 9, 2010

The *nihil obstat* and *imprimatur* are official declarations
that a book is free of doctrinal or moral error.

For additional information on the "Come and See ~ Catholic Bible Study"
series visit www.CatholicBibleStudy.net

Catholic Bible Study

Ezekiel, Hebrews, Revelation

Introduction

Let us then with confidence draw near to the throne of grace,
that we may receive mercy and find grace to help in time of need.
Hebrews 4:16

The Book of Ezekiel is a challenging book to study. It appears to be a well-constructed whole. Its author was a priest, and the temple in Jerusalem was his ruling interest: the temple defiled by pagan rites (Ezekiel 8), the temple deserted by the glory of God (Ezekiel 10), and the temple of the future (Ezekiel 40–48). The Law (Torah) is venerated, and Israel is constantly accused of profaning the sabbaths, a frequent refrain of his indictment of Israel (Ezekiel 20). This priest is also a prophet of action. More than any other prophet, he resorts to symbolic gestures in marked contrast to the simplicity of his predecessors. Not least of all, Ezekiel is a visionary with an extraordinary gift of pictorial imagination. His book contains only four formal visions, but these occupy a substantial part of it, and they admit us to the supernatural world. His entire teaching centers upon inner conversion: we must achieve a new heart and a new spirit (Ezekiel 18:31). Here, as with the free divine gift that precedes repentance, we are near to the theology of grace later developed by Saint Paul and Saint John. Ezekiel also stands at the source of the apocalyptic tradition, and his influence is often perceptible in Daniel and the Book of Revelation.

The Letter to the Hebrews assumes that its readers are familiar with the Old Covenant but that they are Jewish Christians, perhaps even Jewish priests (see Acts 6:7) to judge by the emphasis on public worship and ceremony. Having become Christians, they seem to have left Jerusalem and gone for shelter to some coastal town. They are tired of exile and think longingly of the splendor of the temple worship, which they left behind. Persecution discourages them and they are tempted to go back to Judaism. The letter was written to prevent this from happening (Hebrews 10:19–39). To these weary exiles the author presents Christian life in the perspective of the Exodus, marching to the place of Rest, the Promised Land of heaven, an exodus not led by Moses but by Christ. Saint Paul shows how Jesus, the incarnate Son of God, is our Leader and Priest, higher than the angels and ruler of all things.

The Book of Revelation in many ways succeeds the Old Testament prophets. The distinction is that ancient prophets characteristically received the message by "hearing the word of God" and passed it on by word of mouth, whereas Saint John, the author of the Apocalypse, was given his revelation in a cycle of visions and passed it on in writing. His language is richly symbolic, and the importance of the visions is never in their literal meaning. It can be taken as a rule that every element—persons, places, animals, actions, objects, parts of the body, numbers and measurements, stars, constellations, colors and garments—has symbolic value and in order not to misunderstand the writer's message, one must appreciate the imagery at its true value and translate the images back into the ideas which he intended them to convey. This process includes taking into account the historical events that gave birth to the Book of Revelation, during a period of bitter persecution of Christians. The author's mission is to increase the hope and determination of the infant Church, to persevere until the definitive establishment of the Kingdom of God: *"Behold, I am with you always, to the close of the age"* (Matthew 28:20).

What You Need to Do this Bible Study

To do this Bible Study, you need a Catholic Bible and a *Catechism of the Catholic Church* (CCC). When choosing a Bible, remember that the Catholic Bible contains seventy-three books. If you find Sirach and Tobit in your Bible's table of contents, you have a complete Catholic Bible. The Council of Hippo approved these seventy-three books in AD 393, and this has remained the official canon of Sacred Scripture since the fourth Century. The Council of Trent in 1545 authoritatively reaffirmed these divinely inspired books for inclusion in the canon of the Bible. The Douay-Rheims, one of the first English translations of the Catholic Bible, was completed in 1609.

For Bible study purposes, choose a word-for-word, literal translation rather than a paraphrase. Some excellent translations are the Revised Standard Version Catholic Edition (RSVCE), the Jerusalem Bible (JB), and the New American Bible (NAB). For this study, we highly recommend using the RSVCE, since different translations number verses differently. The RSVCE Bible is quoted in all passages, and has been used in writing the home study questions. If you have difficulty answering a particular question, borrow an RSVCE Bible and you should be able to find the answer to the question.

How To Do This Bible Study

1. Pray to the Holy Spirit to enlighten your mind and spirit.
2. Read the Bible passages for the first chapter.
3. Read the commentary in this book.
4. Use your Bible and Catechism to write answers to the home study questions.
5. Find a small group and share your answers aloud on those questions.
6. Watch the videotape lecture that goes with this study.
7. End with a short wrap-up lecture and/or prayer.

Invite and Welcome Priests and Religious

Ask for the blessing of your pastor before you begin. Invite your pastor, associate pastor, deacon, visiting priests, and religious sisters to participate in this Bible study. Invite priests and religious to come and pray with the Bible study members, periodically answer questions from the question box, or give a wrap-up lecture. Accept whatever they can offer to the Bible study. However, don't expect or demand anything from them. Appreciate that the clergy are very busy and don't add additional burdens on them. Accept with gratitude whatever is offered.

Practical Needs

❋ Ask God for wisdom about whom to study with, where, and when to meet.
❋ Gather a small prayer group to pray for your Bible study and your specific needs. Pray to discern God's will in your particular situation.
❋ Show this book to your pastor and ask for his approval and direction.
❋ Choose a day of the week and time to meet.
❋ Invite neighbors and friends to a "Get Acquainted Coffee" to find out who will make a commitment to meet for 60 to 90 minutes each week for Bible study.
❋ Find an appropriate location. Start in someone's home or in the parish hall if the space is available and the pastor will allow it.
❋ Hire a babysitter for mothers with young children and share the cost amongst everyone, or find some volunteers to provide childcare.
❋ Consider a cooperative arrangement, in which women take turns caring for the children. All women, even grandmothers and women without children, should take turns, serving the children as an offering to God.

Pray that God will anoint specific people to lead your study. Faithful, practicing Catholics are needed to fill the following positions:

❋ **Teachers**—take responsibility to read commentaries and prepare a fifteen to twenty minute wrap-up lecture after the small group discussion and video.
❋ **Song Leaders**—lead everyone in singing a short hymn to begin Bible study.
❋ **Prayer Leaders**—open Bible study with a short prayer.
❋ **Children's Teachers**—teach the young children who come to Bible study.
❋ **Coordinators**—communicate with parish personnel about needs for rooms, microphones, and video equipment. Make sure rooms are left in good shape.
❋ **Small Group Facilitators** will be needed for each small group. Try to enlist two mature Catholics who are good listeners to serve together as co-leaders for each small group and share the following responsibilities:

❖ Pray for each member of your small group every day.
❖ Make a nametag for each member of the group.
❖ Meet before the study to pray with other leaders.
❖ Discuss all the questions in the lesson each week.
❖ Begin and end on time.
❖ Make sure that each person in the group shares each week. Ask each person to read a question and have the first chance to answer it.
❖ In the discussion group you could go around in a circle, so that each person can look forward to his or her turn to read a question. After reading the question, the reader can answer the question or pass, and then others can feel free to add additional comments.
❖ Make sure that no one person dominates the discussion, including you!
❖ Keep the discussion positive and focused on the week's lesson.

- Speak kindly and charitably. Steer conversation away from any negative or uncharitable speech, gossip, or griping. Don't badmouth anyone or any church.
- Listen well! Keep your ears open and your eyes on the person speaking.
- Give your full attention to the one speaking. Be comfortable with silence. Be patient. Encourage quieter people to share first. Ask questions.
- If questions, misunderstandings, or disagreements arise, refer them to the question box for a teacher to research or the parish priest to answer later.
- Arrange for a social activity each month.

Logistical Considerations

- Jesus chose a group of twelve apostles. So, perhaps twelve or thirteen people make the best small groups. When you get too many, break into two groups.
- A group of teenagers or a young adult group could be facilitated by the parish priest or a young adult leader.
- Men share best with men and women with women. If you have a mixed Bible study, organize separate men's groups led by men and women's groups led by women. In mixed groups, some people tend to remain silent.
- Offer a married couples' group, if two married couples are willing to lead the group. Each person should have his or her own book.

- Sit next to the most talkative person in the group and across from the quietest. Use eye contact to affirm and encourage quieter people to speak up. Serve everyone and hear from everyone.
- Listening in Bible study is just as important as talking. Evaluate each week. Did everyone share? Am I a good listener? Did I really hear what others shared? Was I attentive or distracted? Did I affirm others? Did I talk too much?

- Share the overall goal aloud with all of the members of the group. We want to hear from each person in the group, sharing aloud each time the group meets.
- Make sure that people share answers only on those questions on which they have written down answers. Don't just share off the top of your head. Really study.

- Consider a nursing mothers' group in which mothers can bring their infants and hold them while sharing their home study questions.
- Family groups can work together on a family Bible study night, reading the commentary and scriptures aloud and helping one another to find answers in the Bible and Catechism.
- Parents or older siblings can read to young children and help the youngsters to do the crafts in the children's Bible study book.

Social Activities

God has created us as social creatures, needing to relate communally. Large parishes make it difficult for people to get to know one another. Some people can belong to a parish for years without getting to know others. Newcomers may never get noticed and welcomed. Bible study offers an opportunity for spiritual nourishment as well as inclusion and hospitality. Occasional social activities are recommended in this book. These socials are simple, fun, and easy. In planning your social activities be a good sport and try to attend with your group.

* Agree on a time when most of the group can meet. This could be right before or after Bible study or a different day of the week, perhaps even Saturday morning.
* Invite people to come to your home for the social time. Jesus was comfortable visiting the homes of the rich and the poor. So, whatever your circumstances, as a Christian you can offer hospitality to those God sends along your way.

> *Do not neglect to show hospitality to strangers,*
> *for thereby some have entertained angels unawares.*
> *(Hebrews 13:2)*

* Keep it simple! Just a beverage and cookies work well. Simplicity blesses others. People can squeeze together on a sofa or stand around the kitchen. Don't fuss.
* Help the group leader. If Bible study meets in someone's home, invite the group to come to your place for the social time. Don't make the group leader do it all.
* If Bible study meets at church, don't have all of the socials at church as well. Try to have some fellowship times in people's homes. Perhaps over the Christmas break you can go to someone's home for coffee and cookies after Christmas and before Bible study starts up again.

Suggested Times for Socials

9:30–10:30 a.m.	Saturday coffee	12:00–1:00 p.m.	Luncheon
3:00–4:00 p.m.	Afternoon tea	8:00–9:00 p.m.	Dessert

Modify times to meet your specific needs. If your parish has Saturday morning Mass at 9:00 a.m., adjust the time of your social to accommodate those members of the group who would like to attend Mass and need some time to get to the social. If lunch after Bible study makes too long of a day for children who need naps, plan the social for a different day. A mother's group might meet after school when high school students are available to baby-sit.

Class Schedule

Accept responsibility for being a good steward of time. God gives each of us twenty-four hours every day. If Bible study starts or ends late, busy people may drop out. Late starts punish the prompt and encourage tardiness. Be a good steward of time. Begin and end Bible study with prayer at the agreed upon time. If people consistently arrive late or leave early, investigate whether you have chosen the best time for most people. You may have a conflict with the school bus schedule or the parish Mass schedule. Perhaps beginning a few minutes earlier or later could be a service to those mothers who need to pick up children from school.

Possible Bible Study Class Schedules

MORNING CLASS

9:30 a.m.	Welcome, song, prayer
9:40 a.m.	Video
9:55 a.m.	Small group discussion
10:40 a.m.	Wrap-up lecture and prayer

AFTERNOON CLASS

1:00 p.m.	Welcome, song, prayer
1:10 p.m.	Small group discussion
1:55 p.m.	Video
2:10 p.m.	Wrap-up lecture and prayer

EVENING CLASS

7:30 p.m.	Welcome, song, prayer
7:40 p.m.	Small group discussion
8:25 p.m.	Video
8:40 p.m.	Wrap-up lecture and prayer

As you can see, the video could be shown either before or after the small group discussion, and either before, after, or instead of a wrap-up lecture. Whether or not you choose to use the videotapes, please begin and end with prayer.

Wrap-Up Lecture

Additional information is offered in videotaped lectures, which are available for this study and can be obtained from Emmaus Road Publishing Company, 827 North Fourth Street, Steubenville, Ohio, 43952. You can obtain DVDs of these lectures by going to www.emmausroad.org on the Internet or by calling 1-800-398-5470. Videotaped lectures may be used in addition to, or in place of a wrap-up lecture, depending on your needs.

When offering a closing lecture, the presenter should spend extra time in prayer and study to prepare a good, sound lecture. The lecturer should consult several Catholic Bible study commentaries and prepare a cohesive, orthodox lecture. Several members of the leaders' team could take turns giving wrap-up lectures. Also, invite priests, deacons, and religious sisters to give an occasional lecture.

The lecturer should:
* Be a faithful, practicing Catholic. Seek spiritual direction. Frequent the sacraments, especially the Eucharist and Reconciliation.
* Obtain the approval and blessing of your parish priest to teach.
* Use several different presenters whenever possible.
* Pray daily for all of the leaders and members of the study.
* Pray over the lesson to be studied and presented.

* Outline the Bible passages to be studied.
* Identify the main idea of the Bible study lesson.
* Find a personal application from the lesson. How can one make a practical response to God's word?
* Plan a wrap-up lecture with a beginning, a middle, and an end.
* Use index cards to keep focused. Don't read your lecture; talk to people.

* Proclaim, teach, and reiterate the teachings of the Catholic Church. Learn what the Catholic Church teaches, and proclaim the fullness of truth.
* Illustrate the main idea presented in the passage by using true stories from the lives of the saints, or the lives of contemporary Christians.
* Use visuals—a flip chart or overhead transparencies if possible.
* Plan a skit, act out a Bible story, and interact with the group.

* Try to make the scriptures come alive for the people in your group.
* Provide a question box. Find answers to difficult questions or ask a parish priest to come and answer questions on occasion.
* When difficult or complex personal problems arise or are shared in the group, seek out the counsel of a priest.
* Begin and end on time. When you get to the end of your talk, stop and pray.

Challenges

"All scripture is inspired by God and profitable for teaching, for reproof, for correction, and for training in righteousness, that the man of God may be complete, equipped for every good work" (2 Timothy 3:16–17).

As Christians, all of us are weak and need God's mercy and forgiveness. Lay groups can attract people with problems and challenges. Don't try to be all things for all people. Jesus is the Savior, and we are only His servants. When problems loom, direct them to a priest or counselor. Bible study demands faithfulness to the one task at hand, while praying for others in their needs. Saint Paul encourages us to *"speak the truth in love... and be kind to one another, tenderhearted, forgiving one another, as God in Christ forgave you"* (Ephesians 4:15,32). Bible study provides the opportunity for us to search God's word for direction in our personal lives and to pray for, encourage, and sometimes gently admonish one another.

> To interpret Scripture theologically means not only to listen to the historical authors whom it juxtaposes, even opposes, but to see the one voice of the whole, to seek the inner identity that sustains the whole and binds it together... Scripture is interpreted by Scripture... The reading of Scripture as a unity thus logically entails... reading it as something present, not only in order to learn about what was once the case or what people once thought, but to learn what is true... The question of truth is a naïve, unscientific question. And yet, it is the real question of the Bible as such... The question is meaningful only if the Bible itself is something present, if a subject stands apart from all other living historical subjects, because it is bound up with the truth and, therefore, can convey knowledge of the truth in human speech.
> Pope Benedict XVI, *Mary, The Church at the Source,* [with Han Urs Van Balthasar] (San Francisco, CA: Ignatius Press, 1977)p. 39–41.

A Prayer to the Holy Spirit

O Holy Spirit, Beloved of my soul, I adore You,
enlighten, guide, strengthen and console me.
Tell me what I ought to say and do,
and command me to do it.

I promise to be submissive in everything You will ask of me
and to accept all that You permit to happen to me,
only show me what is Your will.

(Joseph Cardinal Mercier)

Chapter 1
Call of the Prophet
Ezekiel 1–3

"Son of man, I have made you a watchman for the house of Israel;
whenever you hear a word from my mouth, you shall give them warning from me.
If I say to the wicked, 'You shall surely die,' and you give him no warning,
nor speak to warn the wicked from his wicked way, in order to save his life,
that wicked man shall die in his iniquity;
but his blood I will require at your hand.
But if you warn the wicked, and he does not turn from his wickedness,
or from his wicked way, he shall die in his iniquity;
but you will have saved your life …
Nevertheless if you warn the righteous man not to sin, and he does not sin,
he shall surely live, because he took warning;
and you will have saved your life."
Ezekiel 3:17–19, 21

The prophet Ezekiel (his name in Hebrew means "God is strong" or "God strengthens") is one of the most difficult prophets of the Old Testament. He is the most visual with numerous visions bringing about the symbolic style of writing found in the book. Ezekiel, son of Buzi from a priestly family of the line of Zadok, prophesied in Babylon during the exile from about 598 to 571 BC after the fall of Jerusalem. Jeremiah and Ezekiel did not exaggerate in their descriptions of the moral and religious depravity, which made chastisement inevitable and sealed the fate of Jerusalem and Judah.

Not having access to the temple anymore, the focus of Israel's religion is shifted to the Word of God. Ezekiel is part of that Word of God, in his visions describing God's plan for His chosen people. The prophet's mission was to the exiles in Babylon, maintaining monotheistic worship among them and reminding them to avoid idolatry. Ezekiel's mission was obstructed during a long period of time because of the people's rebellious and incredulous character, their presumption and despair. This is why supernatural manifestations, symbolic actions, parables and popular sayings were particularly necessary to excite interest and attention. Not least, the visions taught them that the dominion of God extended beyond the land of his own people to all parts of the world.

The various lessons on personal responsibility and divine mercy, including the promise to resuscitate the nation, counteracted the exiles' despair. The repeated descriptions of the sins of Israel in all its history and in all classes of its population were intended to show them that their punishment was just.

Ezekiel's book can be divided into three main parts: (1) threats of punishment against Jerusalem and Judah, Ezekiel 1–24, (2) prophecies against Gentile neighbors, Ezekiel 25–32, and (3) promises of a restoration of the exiles, Ezekiel 33–48. Prominent in his book is the notion of God as the Holy One, remote and transcendent, who in turn demands holiness in His people through obedience to covenant laws and observance of liturgy. In fact, the motif given for Israel's restoration is vindication of God's Holy Name. At the same time, Ezekiel is an eloquent commentator of the need of interior religion. One of his greatest contributions is his stress on personal responsibility for sin, indicating that God is not unjust in reproving rebellious Israel.

The prophet sees two distinct future events, the proximate national revivification and a remote establishment of the messianic kingdom, which eventually become conjoined, causing his messianism to be so markedly national and material. The future Messiah is viewed as a Good Shepherd, the sprout of the dried-up trunk of the tree of David, and above all as a new David. After defeating His enemies He will reign in a kingdom of peace, the assurance of the Lord's protection. A centerpiece of that reign is a splendid temple, a mysterious reproduction of Solomon's temple. Entry into the kingdom requires sincere conversion, a new heart and a new spirit.

Ezekiel's influence is seen in the Apocalypse of Saint John, also known as the book of Revelation. Especially in Ezekiel 40–48, a detailed portrayal of the New Temple, the new cult and the new Holy Land, appear to be an ideal interpretation of Isaiah's New Jerusalem, which then becomes reality in the Apocalypse. Moreover, the apocalyptic visions, for instance, of the Son of Man, of God's throne, of the four living creatures, of a little scroll containing God's eternal designs for creation, of cosmic signs, of angelic apparitions, of marks on the foreheads of the faithful, of measuring the temple, of reviving God's witnesses, of earthquakes, of mourning over the fall of Babylon, of voices like the sound of mighty waters, of Gog and Magog, and of the river of life, all are inspired by this great prophet. His very last word regarding the name of that New City sums up the covenant between God and man: *"The LORD is there"* [Hebrew *YWHW shammá,*] (Ezekiel 48:35)!

This first section of Ezekiel sets the major themes of the book: the presence of the divine glory in the drama of the exile, the vocation of the prophet to be a sentinel on behalf of Israel, the responsibility of each person for his or her actions, and the power of the Word of God despite the people's rebellious refusal to listen and obey. In the current religious crisis, Ezekiel tells Israel that their defeat is due to God's punishment. If, however, they do turn back to Him, He will restore the people and the city after the time of exile.

A Theophany is an appearance of God or a manifestation of the divine—This wondrous vision in Ezekiel 1:1–28 is like a dream perceived in the inner senses of the prophet's mind in an atmosphere of mystery and awe. God appears to Ezekiel in His heavenly chariot, just as the heavens opened at Christ's baptism (Matthew 3:16). The four living creatures who support His throne are first pictured, then the chariot wheels, then the throne, and finally the figure on the throne. The accompanying figures used—

cherubim, anatomical description, the four countenances, and the cosmic features—may be traced back to both Old Testament sources and maybe to the influence of other nations, Babylonian and Canaanite.

Time, place and author are revealed in Ezekiel 1:1–3. The "thirtieth year" may be related to the year of Nebuchadnezzar's reign, or to the prophet's personal age. Other dates mentioned are reckoned from the captivity of Jehoiachin in the first year of Zedekiah, 597 BC, in Nissan (March-April) the first month of the Jewish year. The place is Babylon, the land of the Chaldeans, at Tel-abib, most likely a chief settlement or colony of Jewish deportees. At crucial moments in the history of His chosen people, God directly takes control of the senses and power of speech of His prophet: *"And the hand of the Lord was there upon me"* (Ezekiel 3:22; 8:1–3; 33:22; 37:1; 40:1). Here Ezekiel is being described like Elijah, who was famed for being moved by the hand of the Lord (1 Kings 18:46). Also, the prophet Habakkuk was transported through the air in Daniel 14:36, which is a certain foreshadowing of Christ's ascension into heaven.

A tempest, dark cloud, and fire or lightening usually accompany a *theophany*—this manifestation of the divine on earth. Remember the thunder, lightening and thick cloud that accompanied God's coming to Moses on Mount Sinai in Exodus 19:16. Tellingly, the vision as the harbinger of doom comes from the north, the region of darkness and calamity. From the midst of the fire something gleamed like an amalgam of gold and silver, images of Christ standing between God and humanity.

The cherubim remind us of the two angels of hammered gold that adorned the two ends of the mercy seat of the Ark of the Covenant (Exodus 25:18). And, when Solomon built a temple for the Lord, he embellished the inner sanctuary with two cherubim as well (1 Kings 6:23). The Hebrew calls them *hayyót*, "living creatures" here, and "cherubim" in Ezekiel 9:3 and 10:1. We might explain the "faces" as aspects, but the "wings"—the eagle aspect—are distinguished from the faces in the description, and they enable a face-forward-movement in all four directions. These faces, respectively, seem to express the intelligence (man/angel), strength (ox), majesty (lion), and swiftness (eagle) of the cherubim, and thus reflect in themselves in a sublime way those divine attributes in creation. They are also different aspects of the life of Jesus our Savior. Saint Ambrose sees in them the four cardinal virtues of prudence, justice, fortitude, and temperance.

The jointless legs and rounded soles exclude bending and turning. The text makes a distinction between the living beings and the Spirit that actually moves them, reinforcing the clear sense of the passage that it is the will of the One above them that inspires their motion. Moreover, like the burning bush that signaled a divine presence to Moses (Exodus 3:2–5), the fire and blaze announce the divine nature of this vision and stress the holiness of the scene. As with Moses, the prophet Ezekiel must not interfere but must submit obediently.

The wheels rest on the ground when the chariot comes to earth. Directed by the Spirit of God, wheels and cherubs moved harmoniously in all four directions without turning.

They also indicate the presence of a war chariot and of the Divine Warrior in battle. The many eyes on the wheels' rims reveal the all-seeing Lord of history. The Fathers of the Church interpret the wheels in reference to the scriptures or the work of preaching.

The platform resting above the living beings recalls the firmament (Genesis 1:6), and God's footstool (Exodus 24:10). Its firmness and color are indicated by the comparisons, and it appears to extend as far as the outstretched wings. Above the firmament the figure of a man is enthroned, all fiery and encompassed with a brightness resembling the rainbow. God dwells above the heavens in Israelite cosmology. The *many waters* (Ezekiel 1:24) allude to the primeval deeps symbolizing the powers of chaos opposed to divine order and balance.

"Seated above the likeness of a throne was a likeness as it were of a human form" (Ezekiel 1:26). Words like "likeness" and "appearance" in this biblical genre are employed to safeguard the spirituality of God. The vision appeared to be human but was wrapped in the numinous qualities of fire, splendor, and awesome holiness. Ezekiel identifies this figure with the glory of the Lord *kabód*, the epiphany of the divine majesty of God in Israel. In Exodus 33:23, Moses did not see God's face, but only the "glory" of His back—the only other example of the divine *kabód* in human form. Ezekiel saw only the likeness of the glory of God, not the real glory according to Saint Gregory the Great. The Church Fathers interpret Ezekiel's vision of the human likeness upon the sapphire throne as a prophesy of the Incarnation of the Logos from the Theotokos (Mother of God), the Virgin Mary, who in many ancient church hymns is called the "living Throne of God."

This theophany in Babylonia conveyed a weighty message to the exiles. They shared, to some extent, in the pagan belief that the presence and power of a god were limited to a certain region. By His splendid epiphany in a foreign land Yahweh, the God of Israel, manifested His omnipresence and omnipotence. The deportees in Babylon share the same protective presence of God in their midst as those in the homeland. And when Jerusalem will be destroyed, Israel's hope will remain intact among the exilic community.

Vocation to the prophetic ministry (Ezekiel 2:1–3:27)—God informs Ezekiel of his mission, sets him up as His interpreter and eventually sends him to preach to his fellow-captives at Tel-abib.

The task (Ezekiel 2:1–7)—Ezekiel prostrates himself in fear and reverence before the glory of God. The vision shifts from an overwhelming visual experience to an emphasis on hearing that in many ways resembles the auditory character of Jeremiah's call. A voice bids him rise and he obeys, strengthened by the Spirit. The prophet could not endure a direct experience of God any more than Moses, so the divine empowering is indispensable. Frequently, "the Spirit of the Lord" gives a person extraordinary powers to act superhumanly (Judges 11:29; 14:6), or to become ecstatic and prophesy (1 Samuel 10:10).

Here, the expression *son of man* means simply man. It recurs ninety times in the book, stressing the littleness of man compared with the greatness of God, yet it also underscores the universality of the message to be proclaimed. Judgment and deliverance lie in God's hands, not ours. However, in Daniel 7:13 *son of man* becomes a messianic title. Eventually, in the Gospel of John, we find this title on the lips of Christ as a favorite expression of His Incarnation, marvelously incorporating the idea of the suffering servant of the prophet Isaiah with the eternal transcendence of Daniel's *son of man*. In the Synoptic Gospels, Jesus uses the title *"Son of man"* as well (Matthew 8:20) to refer to Himself. By contrast, the Israelites are portrayed as an intractable nation. The metaphor "to sit upon scorpions" seems to refer to a dwelling among unruly and dangerous men. Saint John Chrysostom sees those scorpions as evil in their hearts.

The message (Ezekiel 2:8–3:3)—The Lord presents the prophet with a written scroll containing lamentation, mourning and woe, commanding him to eat it, as did Jeremiah (Jeremiah 15:16). John on Patmos will repeat that same gesture in Revelation 10:8–11. Moreover, Jeremiah 36 illustrates the reality and usage of a scroll in biblical antiquity. This incident demonstrates that God is the actual source of what Ezekiel preached, and that the divine pronouncements are threats of punishment. The prophet was to make the message completely his own by filling his stomach with it as with real food, like honey to teach us wisdom.

It is important to remember the symbolic character of this vision, affecting the internal senses of a prophet. The way of describing God with human features is called *anthropomorphism*. A hand stretches out to Ezekiel with the scroll, symbolizing God's direct interaction and proximity regarding the human person receiving His revelation. Ezekiel then feels the sweetness of the book, understanding that this message is a gracious gift full of consolations for him and for his listeners. Later on, the prophet will feel the acerbity of the burden. As a fascinating aside, the visionary of Patmos, Saint John, has a similar experience in that the little book swallowed first tastes sweet, but then causes bitterness in his stomach (Revelation 10:10). Origen says that although the scriptures are sweet to the taste, they become bitter when our understanding grows.

The sending (Ezekiel 3:4–15)—The prophet is now sent to the deportees, the recipients of his instructions. Yet God cautions him that his stubborn audience will not comply with his words, and empowers him to carry on against all antagonism. Does this not resemble Jesus' words against Chorazin and Bethsaida in Matthew 11:21 and 12:41? Ezekiel is now fully commissioned to go to the exiles, and a supernatural force uplifts him spiritually and impels him there. Saint John will also be transported "in the Spirit" in Revelation 4:2. His commotion of soul is due to the realization of the imminent trials awaiting him. Exhausted by his experiences he remains overwhelmed for seven days at Tel-abib until a further divine inspiration revives him. Saint Augustine encourages believers to stay firm in the truth regardless of the response of others.

Prophetic accountability (Ezekiel 3:16–21)—Ezekiel is outstanding for his spiritual leadership on personal responsibility, which is a departure from the widespread previous notion of corporate accountability of the Israelites as a collective entity, as a people. Here the issue is considered from the prophet's standpoint. He is compared to a watchman.

The tradition of the prophet being a sentinel predates Ezekiel and can be found in Hosea, Habakkuk and Isaiah. Saint Caesarius opines that this image also applies to the office of bishop.

Both preacher and hearer are individually accountable if no warning is given. The sinner alone is responsible if he does not heed a warning, and the punishment for disobedience is death. *"You shall surely die"* is a classic royal formula for giving the death penalty, delivered by kings (1 Samuel 14:44; 22:16; 1 Kings 2:37) and by God in a cultic setting of law (Genesis 2:17; 2 Kings 1:4, 6). Longevity is the reward for the prophet's faithfulness for the sinner's conversion. Eloquently, the passage reflects first on the chronic sinner, then the upright person who occasionally falls into sin. Conversion is seen as equally necessary in both cases.

Seclusion and silence (Ezekiel 3:22–27)—These verses probably belong to the first cycle of prophecies. The Lord directs Ezekiel to remain in his house and abstain from preaching. From accounts of the elders coming to him (Ezekiel 14:1; 20:1), it seems he did not go out to publicly preach, as Jeremiah was wont to do, but spoke only on occasion from his own home. Apparently he had a considerable reputation that drew people to ask him what God was doing (Ezekiel 33:30ff). What follows is one of the copious symbolic actions ascribed to his ministry. The binding with cords (Hippolytus argues that the cords that bind the prophet are the Babylonians) and attachment of the tongue to the palate serve as illustrations of the withdrawal and wordlessness imposed upon him for seven days, ending only with the fall of Jerusalem (Ezekiel 24:25–27; 33:21ff). God is the initiator of both muteness and confining. It is absolutely unnecessary to see these as physical maladies like aphasia or catalepsy. On the contrary, the motive for the precept was the ineptitude, unworthiness and unpreparedness of the exiles. Finally, it is clear from the whole commissioning scene the silence was not muteness but a restraint placed on the prophet to reinforce that he would speak only words commanded by God.

Again, the Book of Revelation bears several significant traces of the influence of Ezekiel. The vision of the chariot from heaven with the four living creatures (Ezekiel 1:5–10) becomes the heavenly throne room with the four creatures surrounding Christ (Revelation 4:1–8). The prophet is bidden to eat the scroll (Ezekiel 2:8), as is the seer on Patmos (Revelation 10:8–9). The harlot is condemned (Ezekiel 16:23; Revelation 17:1–6, 15–18). And both Ezekiel and Revelation end with a vision of the new temple (Ezekiel 40–48; Revelation 21–22). The four living creatures take on an important symbolic role and are applied by the Fathers to the four Gospels, as well as to other aspects to the life of faith, both cosmological and psychological.

The Vision of Ezekiel

Raphael (1483–1520 AD)

1. Who writes this book, and what prompted him to do so? Ezekiel 1:1–3

2. Describe the four living creatures. Ezekiel 1:4–15

3. What prompted the movement of the four living creatures? Ezekiel 1:20

4. What is above the heads of the living creatures?

Genesis 1:6–8	
Ezekiel 1:22	

5. Describe some characteristics of the following beings:

Genesis 3:24	
Exodus 25:18–22	
1 Samuel 4:4	
Ezekiel 1:22–25	

6. Identify a piece of regal ceremonial furniture in these verses:

Ezekiel 1:26
Revelation 1:4
Revelation 4:2

7. Describe the appearance in the following passages:

Exodus 24:16
Ezekiel 1:26–28

8. What does the vision in Ezekiel 1:26–28 reveal? CCC 1137

9. How does Ezekiel respond to the vision? Ezekiel 1:28–2:1

10. What title does the Lord use to address Ezekiel? Ezekiel 2:1

11. Who enters Ezekiel and what happens? Ezekiel 2:2

12. Explain Ezekiel's commission from God. Ezekiel 2:3–8

* What special job or commission has God given to you?

13. What happens in Ezekiel 2:9–3:3?

14. To whom is Ezekiel sent and what must he do? Ezekiel 3:4–11

15. How did Ezekiel travel? Ezekiel 3:12–15

16. Explain the command given in Ezekiel 3:16–21.

17. What will happen if the watchman doesn't warn the wicked? Ezekiel 3:18

* Has God ever prompted you to confront someone's sin? What happened?

18. What happens if someone doesn't heed a warning? Ezekiel 3:19

19. Explain Ezekiel 3:21 in your own words. How could you do this today?

20. What happens in Ezekiel 3:22–27?

*Is it more difficult for you to keep silent when you should, or to speak up when God seems to be prompting you to do so? In which area could you improve?

Chapter 2
Warnings for Jerusalem
Ezekiel 4–11

And behold, the glory of the God of Israel was there,
like the vision that I saw in the plain.
Ezekiel 8:4

Symbolic announcement of the siege of Jerusalem and the exile—This section of Ezekiel is divided into three symbolic actions with elaborations of their meaning, followed by three programmatic oracles of judgment (Ezekiel 5:5–7:27). The symbolic acts serve as a literary indictment and accusation, while the oracles in chapters 5–7 are short on accusations and long on formal sentencing for Israel's crimes. It all revolves around a basic charge against the people of the sin of idolatry—high treason against God, which will bring a death penalty! The days represented in this text are periods of symbolic expiation referring to the exile. Israel's exile lasted 183 years from 721–538 BC. Judah's exile lasted 49 years from 587–538 BC. The figures 190 and 40 preserved by the Greek Old Testament (the *Septuagint)* are round numbers closely approximating these periods of exile. Also, "Israel" designates the Northern kingdom after Samaria's fall (Ezekiel 11:10–12). Obviously since Ezekiel was ordered to prepare, cook and eat his food in the sight of the exiles, do not suppose that he was literally bound or even paralyzed.

God orders the prophet to take a clay brick or tablet (used in Babylonia for diagrams or writing) and on it portray Jerusalem in a state of siege. The siege wall, which may have been a circle of forts, the mound built up against the city wall, the camps of the besiegers and their battering rams are all depicted. Possibly, the various terms refer to one huge machine or siege tower. The iron wall encircling and isolating the besieged is represented by the iron griddle—normally used for baking bread—which Ezekiel erects between himself and the city. Saint Jerome states that the iron plate signals the barrier between Israel and their God. Then he besieges the city in representation of the Babylonians, menaces it with his bare arm and prophesies against it, predicting future events (Ezekiel 8:1). Ezekiel's actions may seem strange, but are intended by God to instruct the people. Many of these gestures may have been preached and described rhetorically rather than performed.

Famine—Ezekiel is restricted to a daily ration of twenty shekels of bread (about eight ounces) and a sixth of a hin of water (about two pints). Water rationing would be felt particularly in the hot climate of Babylonia. The rationed food is a figure of famine: "*I will break the staff of bread in Jerusalem"* (Ezekiel 4:16).

Unclean foods during the exile—The desperation brought on by famine is depicted in the mixture of wheat and barley, beans and lentils, millet and spelt. This was unlawful just as sowing two kinds of grain in one field or using two kinds of textile for one garment (Leviticus 19:19; Deuteronomy 22:9–11). The prescribed fuel for baking was also unclean and revolting. According to Deuteronomy 23:12–14, human excrement was unclean and was to be kept outside the camp. Ezekiel insists on his priestly fidelity to the Law, which forbids priests to have contact with unclean animals and sacrifices (Leviticus 22:8; 7:18). His prayer obtained a mitigation of this uncleanness. Food eaten in exile was unclean because it was impossible to offer sacrifices and offerings of first fruits by which it was sanctified.

Annihilation of the citizens—This symbolic act of cutting off the beard is inspired by Leviticus 26:33 and Isaiah 7:20. In the first case, God will draw His sword and bring Israel to ruin. In the second, He will employ a foreign power to shave Israel. The last symbol refers to the exile and siege combined. Shaving Judah with a razor indicated the completeness of its devastation (Isaiah 7:20). Here, the order given to Ezekiel signals annihilation of the inhabitants of Jerusalem. Some perish within the city by famine and pestilence, others outside the city by the sword. Still others are deported but shall not escape the sword. A few are spared from the massacre, but not even all of these shall survive. By using a sword, the prophet links the haircutting to killing in battle. Since hair was a sign of strength (Judges 16:17) and dignity (2 Samuel 10:4–5), to be shaved bald was complete humiliation. By joining these prophecies together Ezekiel enhances the threat of total degradation involved.

Explanation of the images (Ezekiel 5:5–17)—The symbols point to the punishment of the inhabitants of Jerusalem for their iniquities. Jerusalem was the religious center of the world. Instead of being an example to the Gentiles, it surpassed them in wickedness; hence its chastisement will be without parallel. *"Thus shall my anger spend itself, and I will vent my fury upon them and satisfy myself"* (Ezekiel 5:13) expresses anthropomorphically God's satisfaction with the completion of His task. Various groups of three dominate the prophet's preaching and actions. The succeeding three oracles in Ezekiel 5:5–17; 6:1–14; and 7:1–27 are closely bound together by triple repetitions. All three use the formula "plague, famine, and sword" (Ezekiel 5:12; 6:11; 7:15), and all decisively state that the evil comes from God's wrath (Ezekiel 5:13–15; 6:12; 7:3).

Announcement of the punishment of Judah (Ezekiel 6:1–14)—The phrase *"the mountains of Israel"* (Ezekiel 6:2) occurs only in Ezekiel, mirroring his disgust with the abuse of the Zion theology, and foreshadowing his concern with the restoration of the mountains of Israel. The high places on the hills were conspicuous centers of idolatrous worship. In the prophet's message they are personified to represent their inhabitants. The shrines of idols are profaned with the bones of their worshippers. These shrines were particularly loathed by the prophets as threats to pure devotion to God (Deuteronomy 12:2; 1 Kings 14:23; Hosea 4:13; Jeremiah 2:20). However, a remnant will be converted after the deportation. Notice here how the comparison of idolatry with marital infidelity emerges in prophetic literature. The image of castigation is tied into the gesture of clapping hands and stamping of feet.

Second announcement of punishment for Judah and Jerusalem (Ezekiel 7:1–27)—This is the third and climactic subject of the divine announcement of judgment in chapters 5 to 7. The sequence has moved Jerusalem to the mountain country, now to the whole land. The theme of the Day of the Lord is traditional among the prophets (Isaiah 13; Amos 5; Zephaniah 1). Having the same subject matter as the previous prophecy, this one emphasizes the imminence, inevitability and enormity of the catastrophe. It may belong to the first year of Ezekiel's ministry. The time, the day, the end has arrived. The four corners of the land indicate the whole of Palestine is affected. The buyer rejoiced in satisfying his desire, the seller regretted the surrender of his possessions, yet now they are equal. The principle is illustrated by the sale of land, which is returned automatically to its original owner in the jubilee year (Leviticus 25:28). The irreparable destruction and the immensity of the disaster appear for the profanation of God's sanctuary and His complete abandonment of His people. God will show neither pity nor mercy. Moreover, the theme of consternation rather than rejoicing is taken directly from Amos 5:18–20, and the whole prophecy may come under the influence of that prophet. Flight to the mountains, like doves of the valley fluttering in terror (Ezekiel 7:16) is a common prophetic image for the horrors of war (Isaiah 16:2; Jeremiah 48:9, 28).

Idolatrous worship in Jerusalem (Ezekiel 8:1–18)—Chapters 8–11 form a unity that is determined by the inclusion of Ezekiel 8:1–3 and Ezekiel 11:22–25, in which the opening and close are made to match. In this vision Ezekiel is transported in spirit to Jerusalem and beholds there:

     1) various forms of idolatry practiced by the citizens,
     2) the slaughter of idolatrous worshippers by avenging angels,
     3) God's abandonment of His city and sanctuary.

These chapters are held together by the progressive stages of divine departure:

     1) the glory of the Lord stands at the inner gate (Ezekiel 8:3),
     2) the presence in the Holy of Holies moves to the threshold (Ezekiel 9:3),
     3) the glory of the Lord moves to the threshold (Ezekiel 10:4),
     4) the glory leaves the city to the east, toward Babylon,
        where He will dwell among the exiles! (Ezekiel 11:23).

Idolatry is evident: Canaanite idol worship, Egyptian animal worship, Tammuz worship from the Babylonians, and Sun worship. The "image of jealousy" set up as God's rival provokes His wrath by receiving the cult of worship due to God alone. This idol was probably Asherah, Baal's consort, originally set up by Manasseh (2 Kings 21:7), removed by Josiah (2 Kings 23:6), and reinstalled by a later king. Josiah's reform, like that of Hezekiah, was followed by an idolatrous reaction. The divine presence will return only when the exiles return (Ezekiel 11:14–21). However, the vision closes with a prediction of restoration.

Egyptian deities were commonly represented as animals. The seventy elders were offering incense, behind closed doors, to various Egyptian gods. According to Exodus 24:1, the elders represent the people of Israel at Mount Sinai, and in Numbers 11:16

they share the spirit of Moses in the community. Here they stand for all Israel guilty of idolatry. Since God seems to have abandoned them when He permitted Josiah's death, the Babylonian depredations, the exile of influential citizens, they would not seek relief from propitiation to foreign gods. Tammuz, the Adonis of the Phoenicians, was a fertility god who was supposed to die in the heat of summer only to return to life in the spring. Further traces of Tammuz cult in Israel can be found is Isaiah 17:10 and Ezekiel 32:19. The women in Ezekiel 8:14 lament his departure to the netherworld.

Ezekiel, led back to the inner court, sees in the space between temple and altar, twenty-five men with their backs to the temple, facing the east and adoring the sun. The number twenty-four is obviously significant to the prophet; it may represent the twenty-four classes of priests who were appointed to serve in the temple in order, with the high priest at their head. Worship of the sun god was known both in Egypt and Mesopotamia. It was also practiced in Israel at the time of Manasseh, since Josiah had to destroy the horses dedicated to the sun found at the temple entrance itself (2 Kings 23:11). Because this is the last in the series of abominations shown to the prophet, it is considered the worst; note that in order to worship the sun, the devotees must turn their back on the Lord! *"Behold, they put the branch to their nose"* (Ezekiel 8:17) suggests an analogy with the Egyptian sun god Re, who is pictured with a vine branch at his nose to signify the transfer of creative power, divine breath, to living things. The sin here is Israel's hypocrisy in committing idolatry while pretending devotion to God.

Punishment of idolaters in Jerusalem (Ezekiel 9)—Ezekiel now beholds six men, representing six angels of ravage who, by God's command, slay all the idolatrous citizens, but spare the innocent who have their foreheads marked with a sign. The *tau* means mark; it is the last letter of the Hebrew alphabet, shaped like a cross. Innocent Israelites were spared by means of this sign as were their forefathers spared long ago in Egypt by means of blood smeared on their doorposts (Exodus 12:21–23; see the parallel episode in Revelation 7:2ff; 9:4). Saint Augustine speaks of an inward sign on the heart, not just the outward sign on the forehead, similar to the indelible signs received in Baptism, Confirmation and Holy Orders. Saint John Chrysostom thought this can also symbolize repentance because of the saving power of the Cross. Here the prophet once more emphasizes personal responsibility for one's moral actions: only the guilty are penalized.

The scribe and six destroyer angels together make seven, the symbolic number of completion, in this case the time of total destruction. They emerge from the upper gate, the north gate of the inner court. Ahaz removed Solomon's bronze altar from the north side of the temple and replaced it with a stone altar (2 Kings 16:14). Ezekiel seems to intercede for the evildoers in Ezekiel 9:8. Manifestations of pity and intercession, however, are unusual in this book; here they intensify the dramatic effect. Even priests are among those to be killed, if they worship idols or can only think of their state, for the inner self reveals the real character of a person.

The prophet introduces into the list of cultic sins and false worship the notion of violence and bloodshed, reflecting the language of the flood narrative in Genesis 6–9, and underscores the fact that this generation, too is deserving of total destruction, as was Noah's.

God's glory leaves Jerusalem (Ezekiel 10)—The glory of the Lord appears, and although the account is incomplete, the novelty in this description is the name *cherubim* given for "living creatures." Also, there is the attribution to the cherubim of the eyes, which adorn the chariot wheels. The spirituality of the cherubim is less apparent here in chapter 10 than it was in chapter 1 of Ezekiel. *"Fill your hands with burning coals from between the cherubim, and scatter them over the city"* (Ezekiel 10:2) foretells the destruction of the city by fire. God returns to the chariot, which then leaves the temple by passing through the east gate. Saint Jerome says that the departure of the glory of God from the temple in Jerusalem leads to the foundation of the Church in Christ.

Judgment against the wicked (Ezekiel 11)—Ezekiel announces the punishment of the wicked counselors in Jerusalem and the restoration of the exiles in Babylonia. Two episodes are similarly introduced by proverbial sayings, which express the false security of the wicked citizens of Jerusalem and their contempt for the exiles.

In Ezekiel 11:1–13, the prophet sees twenty-five of the chief men devising evil counsel at the east gate of the city. They declare themselves protected from destruction by the city wall, as meat in a cauldron is protected from consumption by the fire. Ezekiel states that the corpses of those for whom they are responsible will remain within the wall like meat in a cauldron, and that they themselves shall be deported and slain by the sword (Jeremiah 52:24–27; 2 Kings 25:18–21). The image of the cauldron is used later in Ezekiel 24:1–14 in a different sense.

Who will own the land of God?—The inhabitants of Jerusalem insist: *"They [the exiles] have gone far from the LORD; to us this land is given for a possession"* (Ezekiel 11:15). But, Ezekiel announces that they themselves will be removed from Palestine, while the despised exiles shall return to it, purify it, and possess it as God's people. *"And I will give them one heart, and put a new spirit within them"* (Ezekiel 11:19) predicts that God will renew both the nation and individuals. Saint John Cassian, one of the desert fathers, saw in this passage that any impetus or tendency to goodness on our part would be at God's initiative. Saint Augustine believed that God would give each of us a heart of true understanding. And Saint Barnabas said that the heart of flesh is supremely manifested in Jesus Christ.

At the conclusion of Ezekiel's vision, God abandons Jerusalem. The heavenly chariot appears last on Mount Olivet, where Saint Jerome tells us that Christ would later ascend into heaven. The cherubim lifted up their wings as a sign of the worship offered by all peoples in the future, according to Eusebius. The final hope is that the people are to be restored to their land in order to be God's people in a definitive way.

1. How does God reveal the duration of the exile? Ezekiel 4:1–8

2. What images represent famine and devastation? Ezekiel 4:9–17

3. How does God punish the people? Ezekiel 5:1–12

4. Identify the grave sin found in Ezekiel 6:4–9.

* List some forms of idolatry that distract people from God today.

5. By what three means will the people be put to death? Ezekiel 6:12

6. How does God punish us? Ezekiel 7:8

* Describe a way in which a person is punished according to his ways today.

7. What abomination is occurring in the temple? Ezekiel 8:1–7

8. What idolatrous things are the people worshipping in Ezekiel 8:10–12?

9. Who and how are they worshipping a Babylonian god of fertility in Ezekiel 8:14?

10. What does God use to mark and protect His faithful believers?

Exodus 12:21–23
Ezekiel 9:4–6
Revelation 7:3
CCC 1296

11. What does Ezekiel do in Ezekiel 9:8?

12. Who else gives an example of interceding before God? CCC 2635

* What kind of an intercessor are you? Do you pray for others faithfully?

* Who would you ask to pray for you when you have a need?

13. Identify some reasons for punishment in Ezekiel 9:9.

14. What common characteristic of God is shown in these verses?

Psalm 51:1	
Ezekiel 9:10	

* Describe a time in recent history when God seemed to withhold his mercy.

15. Identify passages that describe the glory of the Lord.

Ezekiel 10:4
Ezekiel 10:18
Ezekiel 10:19

16. What indicates that fire will cause the destruction? Ezekiel 10:2

17. Identify the sin found in Ezekiel 11:2.

18. What must Ezekiel prophesy against the wicked counselors? Ezekiel 11:4–12

19. What hope does God offer in Ezekiel 11:17–18?

20. How does God renew His faithful ones?

Ezekiel 11:19
CCC 715

* Describe a time in your life when you felt God renewing your spirit.

Monthly Social Activity

This month, your small group will meet for coffee, tea, or a simple breakfast, lunch, or dessert in someone's home. Pray for this social event and for the host or hostess. Try, if at all possible, to attend.

After a short prayer and some time for small talk, write a few sentences about some things in your life that have made you very proud. Make sure that everyone has time to share.

Examples

◆ *My parents provided me with music lessons, and I am very pleased that I learned to play piano.*

◆ *My husband raved about the spaghetti and meatballs he enjoyed in his high school cafeteria. I was able to find a recipe and replicate them in a way that made him very pleased.*

◆ *Even though I was never able to go to college, I have always enjoyed reading. People tell me that I am very well read.*

Chapter 3

Exile and Devastion
Ezekiel 12–19

"The soul that sins shall die.
The son shall not suffer for the iniquity of the father,
nor the father suffer for the iniquity of the son;
the righteousness of the righteous shall be upon himself,
and the wickedness of the wicked shall be upon himself."
Ezekiel 18:20

Exile and devastation (Ezekiel 12)—Using symbolic acts Ezekiel foretells (1) the exile in general and the fate of Zedekiah in particular, and (2) the devastation of the land. The prophet's unusual actions would serve to arouse the curiosity of the unbelieving exiles. He makes public preparation for departure in the daytime by collecting his belongings and putting them outside his dwelling. While the people look on he departs by night, passing through a hole he has made in the wall of the city, and with his hand covering his face, possibly a simulation of blindness. This would be a forewarning of what would happen to Zedekiah, who fled Jerusalem through the south-east gate but was captured and blinded before he was led into exile. The second symbolic action, eating and drinking publicly with obvious anxiety, depicts fear of starvation caused by the coming siege.

Prophecy and prophets—Ezekiel here refutes popular sayings about prophecy, and then inveighs against false prophets and prophetesses. Eventually he sets down conditions for obtaining answers from God through a prophet. Ezekiel gives several proverbs about prophets. *"The days grow long and every vision comes to nothing"* (Ezekiel 12:22) scoffs at prophets for unfulfilled prophecies. Time passes but their predictions do not come to pass. God replies that Ezekiel's prophetical threats will be fulfilled immediately, thus giving the lie to the saying. A second adage in Ezekiel 12:27–28 points to the destruction of Judah and Jerusalem. This prophecy will be fulfilled without delay, not after many days and in times far off.

False prophets (Ezekiel 13)—are defined as *"those who prophesy out of their own minds"* (Ezekiel 13:2), announcing to the people their own thoughts and wishes as the words of God, but having seen nothing, that is lacking in supernatural vision. They are like foxes in ruins, undermining instead of building up; like whitewashers of a wall, hiding instead of repairing weaknesses. Their punishment will be exclusion from the people and the land of Israel. Not to be recorded in the register of the house of Israel (Ezekiel 13:9) means rejection. If special meaning is to be given to individual terms in the figure of speech (Ezekiel 13:10–13), the wall may be the false belief that God would protect Jerusalem unconditionally, and the storm may be seen as the Babylonian military invasion. True and false prophets are alive in the Church today as well, and Saint Jerome tells us that we must not be a law unto ourselves. Saint Gregory the Great says that the authentic prophet speaks out against worldly ways. Saint Ambrose warns Christians to flee the false peace of sinners, and Saint Augustine warns against the whitewashed wall of hypocrisy.

The false prophetesses not only attributed to God their own inventions when prophesying in His name, but even adopted Babylonian magical practices. They made bands for their hands and veils for the head to be used as amulets to avert evil influences. Superstitious belief in the efficacy of these talismans purported to give the power of life and death to their dispensers. Prophetesses appear to have preyed upon souls, promising length of life to the sinner who bought their charms and threatened with death the just who refused them. Thus they profaned the one God by prophesying falsely in His name: justice not magic gives length of life! Origen said that the face of the prophet must be properly directed, and his words must avoid superficiality or the distortion of truth. Saint Ambrose reminds us that the true prophet is Jesus Christ!

Idol worshipers consult Ezekiel (Ezekiel 14:1–11)—Ezekiel is ordered to menace them with extermination unless they renounce idolatry, and not to answer their queries under penalty of sharing their fate. Their idolatry seems to have been both internal and external. *"Son of man, these men have taken their idols into their hearts"* (Ezekiel 14:3). God's purpose is their salvation through repentance. Furthermore, the prophet who allows himself to be seduced and answers the demands of idolaters will be extirpated along with them. *"I, the LORD, have deceived that prophet"* (Ezekiel 14:9). For the ancient Israelites, who had no concept of secondary causality, every action good or bad was attributed to God. Today, we would speak of the deception happening with God's permission. Hypocrisy is inflicted upon ourselves alone, when we cannot tell the difference between the exterior and the interior person.

Total corruption of Judah and Jerusalem (Ezekiel 14:12–16:63)—Ezekiel first describes the justice of God in punishing sinful nations, and then the sinfulness of Israel, unfruitful vine and unfaithful spouse. Israel's chastisement, severe and inevitable, will be followed, however, by restoration.

Justice of God's punishment (Ezekiel 14:12–23)—When God penalizes a nation, He spares the just, but not their sons and daughters. In the punishment of Jerusalem, however, some will escape into exile to reveal by their manner of life the justice of God's judgment. Hereby the general law of personal accountability admits exceptions. Just as some of the guilty are spared here, so some of the just will perish with the wicked (see Ezekiel 21:3). Three examples of just men appear in Ezekiel 14:14—Noah lived amid widespread corruption; Job and Daniel remained just in a pagan milieu. The conduct of the fugitives must have been evil to convince earlier deportees of the justice of the castigation. Saint Clement of Rome tells us that there is no substitute for repentance, which is like surgery, in that it inflicts pain but brings about ultimate good.

Jerusalem, the unfruitful vine (Ezekiel 15)—Elsewhere in the Bible, Israel is compared to a cultivated vine of the vineyard (Isaiah 5:1–7; Jeremiah 2:21), which fails to respond to the care of the cultivator and produce fruit. Here, Israel is compared to the wild vine of the forest, which is good for nothing except to be used as fuel for the fire. Both ends of the vine, Israel and Judah, have been burnt. *"Behold, it is given to the fire for fuel; when the fire has consumed both ends of it, and the middle of it is charred, is it useful for anything?"* (Ezekiel 15:4). Only a charred center remains, namely Jerusalem, in which any sap of life survives. But God will complete the ruin.

Jerusalem, the unfaithful spouse (Ezekiel 16)—God cares for Israel as a child, a vivid allegory with a traditional theme: Israel's idolatry is compared to harlotry. Ezekiel presents Israel as a foundling. The previous owners of the land are her parents in that Israel learned their iniquity. The Amorites are Semitic immigrants who invaded Canaan in the nineteenth century BC and could be identified with the Canaanites. The Hittites are the non-Semitic people to the north who invaded the land later on. These people are the pre-Israelitic inhabitants of Canaan. From them Israel absorbed not only some of their racial traits but also some of their pagan rituals and customs. The Early Church Fathers see an allegory on our journey for faith here. Spiritual rebirth in Baptism means cleansing. We need spiritual clothing as we move forward in spiritual growth. Saint Jerome sees the blood alluding to our redemption in Christ. Saint Ephrem sees the paradox of God's love and our rejection of Him played out in the life of Jesus. Saint Gregory the Great challenges us to stand firm against temptation, especially the temptation of pride.

Following Israel's childhood comes adolescence and then betrothal. *"I spread my skirt over you, and covered your nakedness"* (Ezekiel 16:8) means betrothal. In the Book of Ruth, the widow says to Boaz *"I am Ruth, your maidservant; spread your garment over your maidservant, for you are next of kin"* (Ruth 3:9). The Covenant was an espousal between God and His chosen people. Sacrificing God's children to placate false gods was the height of abomination. Infants were first slain and then burned as holocausts to Moloch at Jerusalem (2 Kings 16:3; 17:17; Jeremiah 7:31). In illustrating the crimes of Judah, Ezekiel here brings up foreign worship introduced by alien alliance. Hezekiah made the first treaty with Egypt with the Kushite Pharaoh and later was punished by Sennacherib's invasion. Many cities were detached from Judah and incorporated into the Assyrian province of Ashdod. Yet, Judah differed from ordinary harlots in that she sought for and paid her lovers instead of being sought after and paid by them. Saint Pacian says that heretics follow this corrupt example of the adulterous woman.

The extent of the chastisement of Jerusalem emerges in Ezekiel 16:35–43. Israel will be handed over defenseless to her paramours who will strip her of everything, and as God's appropriate agents will execute on her the sentence pronounced on adulteresses and shedders of blood—death, the penalty for human sacrifice (Ezekiel 16:36). Judah has been fickle in adopting and abandoning false gods. The adulteress is eventually stoned; the murderess has her own blood shed. "Women" here means nations, and particularly Judah's neighbors who rejoiced in her humiliation. Saint Cassian comments that God's anger is not a mark of human rage, but rather a sign of His deep love for us, since we need to be corrected and punished in order to restore our relationship and grow closer to our Creator.

Jerusalem is compared to Samaria and Sodom, confirming the justice of the sentence passed over her (Ezekiel 16:44–58). God's chosen people sinned more than Samaria and Sodom. Since Sodom and Samaria have been punished (Sodom through the cataclysm that destroyed it in Genesis 19:24–25, and Samaria through Assyrian exile), Israel too must be chastened. Israel imitated her heathen Hittite mother, adopted Canaanite gods and offered them human sacrifices. But God will restore both Sodom and Samaria (Ezekiel 16:53), and, unexpectedly, God will restore Jerusalem as well. Restoration and redemption is the hope of all people. Ultimately, Christ is the source of salvation for all of humanity. The name "Sodom" came to be used proverbially of great perversity (Isaiah 1:9ff, Matthew 10:15; 11:23ff), and the same would now be true of Jerusalem. Origen sees the division of the kingdom of Israel as a foreshadowing of the schisms in the Church, caused by pride, the greatest of all sins.

The everlasting Covenant (Ezekiel 16:59–63)—God will re-establish Jerusalem and offer a New Covenant to His chosen people. Israel had broken her oath and violated her covenant from Mount Sinai. After Israel has expiated her crimes, God will establish a New Covenant with her out of His sheer benevolence. The New Covenant will be far greater than the old; indeed it will be eternal (Hosea 2:19–24; Jeremiah 31:33). The New Covenant will embrace all nations, here symbolized by Samaria and Sodom (Psalm 87; Isaiah 2:3; 60:3ff; 66:8ff). The New Covenant would be fully realized in the Church of the new dispensation (Romans 9:1–8; Galatians 4:26ff), and in her divine Founder, Jesus Christ, the Son of God. Restoration is promised, since God cannot remain angry forever.

The Allegory of an eagle, fall of Zedekiah, and advent of the Messiah—A parable to arouse interest appears in Ezekiel 17:1–10. The eagle is Nebuchadnezzar who deposed Jehoichin and enthroned Zedekiah, compared to a well-watered willow shoot comfortably established in Jerusalem. Since his rule was weak he is likened to the lowly vine. The second eagle is Pharaoh Hophra. Nebuchadnezzar dominated the Middle East during the sixth century BC. Though he eventually destroyed the temple in Jerusalem, in Jewish tradition he was used as God's instrument to punish Judah's apostasy, and thus he is often treated positively in the Bible. In the book of Daniel he is portrayed as a wise pagan king who was deceived by evil counselors but was ready to recognize the superiority of Israel's God.

The parable is an allegory explaining the sin and punishment of Zedekiah. By violating his solemn oath of allegiance he offended God and broke faith with Nebuchadnezzar. In the ancient Near East oaths were considered inviolable; yet vassal oaths were often broken, seemingly without qualms, when taken in the name of local gods. Ezekiel is resolute against breaking oaths taken in God's name.

The messianic King will sprout from the Davidic tree (Isaiah 11:1). The goodly cedar is a type of the Messiah, unlike Zedekiah the lowly vine. He becomes a magnificent cedar planted on the heights of Zion. His kingdom is universal, and all nations find shelter therein (Matthew 13:31ff), and all kings recognize its divine origin. The Church is a spacious community according to Origen, and God's nature is to exalt and humble.

Personal responsibility (Ezekiel 18)—There was a mistaken notion that children are punished for the sins of their parents. However, each individual is responsible only for his own transgressions. And if the just man sin or the sinner be converted, neither the former's good deeds nor the latter's evil actions will be remembered. Ezekiel invites all to true repentance, assuring them of the Lord's mercy. God is more eager to pardon than to punish. This teaching on personal accountability and divine mercy was particularly necessary when national responsibility and divine justice led to despair. Although Ezekiel was suffering unjust exile, he of all the prophets stresses the responsibility of every man answering for his own faults.

The proverb *"The fathers have eaten sour grapes, and the children's teeth are set on edge"* (Ezekiel 18:2) claims self-righteously that this generation is being punished for the sins of their forebears, implying that God is unjust. But, Ezekiel says that whoever observes God's commandments is just and will not die prematurely. God's mercy to the repentant sinner and the need of perseverance in the practice of justice complete his teaching. He then gives an urgent invitation to conversion, as John the Baptist will do later on. Saint Ambrose speaks of three kinds of death: the death of sin, the mystical death of Baptism, and physical death. Saint Caesarius says that repentance is a gift; and we should repent now without delay. Saint Clement of Alexandria explains that Christ, the sinless One, delights in the conversion of sinners. And Cassiodorus, a fifth century monk and statesman, affirms that the prayer of confession is one prayer that will always be answered by God.

Elegy on the princes of Israel—The lamentation found in Ezekiel 19 aptly concludes the second cycle of prophecies. This is a highly poetical composition found again in Ezekiel 26:17ff and Ezekiel 27:3–9, 25ff. Its Hebrew name is *quîna*, meaning mournful chant. This particular lamentation is also a parable: two princes are represented as young lions, sons of a lioness, and a third as a vine-branch. Probably Zedekiah is the vine-branch, and the lions are Jehoahaz who was deported to Egypt, and Jehoiachin who was exiled to Babylon. The lioness seems to refer to Judah in the midst of foreign nations. The entire figure of the lion may derive from *"Judah is a lion's whelp"* (Genesis 49:9), containing the symbolism of David's house. The verses also predict Zedekiah's deposition and the exile. Zedekiah is made responsible for the tragedy, and without shoots he can have no successor. Conditions in any family or society in history can cause one to want to mourn and lament. Lamentation can express the sorrow that leads to repentance, redemption, and restoration.

1. What is the prophet foretelling in Ezekiel 12:1–16?

2. Describe what will happen in Ezekiel 12:17–18.

3. Who is condemned in Ezekiel 13:1–7?

4. What is the Lord planning to do, and why in Ezekiel 13:8–16?

5. Who is addressed in Ezekiel 13:17–23? What is the offense?

* What is a contemporary title for a woman described in Ezekiel 13:18?

6. Explain the sins involved in Ezekiel 14:1–7.

7. Describe some upright persons in the Bible.

Ezekiel 14:14	
Hebrews 7:1–3	
CCC 58	

* Describe three contemporary great figures in the faith.

8. What types of punishments afflict people and why? Ezekiel 14:21–23

9. Why does God punish people? Ezekiel 15:7–8

* List some ways in which people are punished unjustly today.

* Now describe some ways in which people receive just punishment today.

10. What can you learn about the following?

Ezekiel 16
CCC 219
CCC 1611

11. Find some hope found in Ezekiel 16:59–63.

12. Describe the allegory in Ezekiel 17:1–10.

13. Now explain the meaning found in Ezekiel 17:11–21.

14. What hope emerges in the following verses?

Isaiah 2:1–4	
Isaiah 11:1	
Ezekiel 17:22–24	

15. Explain the concept of personal responsibility.

Jeremiah 31:29–30	
Ezekiel 18:1–32	
CCC 2056	

16. Put Ezekiel 18:20 into your own words.

* In contemporary society, people often "blame others" for their weaknesses and failings. Give three examples of this phenomenon.

17. What can you learn about God from these verses?

Lamentations 3:22–24
Lamentations 3:31–33
Ezekiel 18:32
Ezekiel 36:24–33

18. What is a lamentation? Ezekiel 19:1   Use a dictionary if necessary.

19. Who could the lioness be?

Genesis 49:9
Ezekiel 19:1–2

20. Write your own Prayer of Lament about something that makes you sad.

Chapter 4
Israel's Infidelity
Ezekiel 20–24

"I the LORD am your God; walk in my statutes,
and be careful to observe my ordinances,
and hallow my sabbaths that they may be a sign between me and you,
that you may know that I the LORD am your God."
Ezekiel 20:19–20

Israel's past and present sins, and future restoration—In August 591 BC, the elders of Tel-abib, Israel's place of exile, ask Ezekiel to consult the Lord for them, and once more Ezekiel tells them that God will neither listen to them nor reply. Instead he recalls the wrongdoing of Israel and the need for its repentance. The Covenant of Sinai was based on monotheism. The Israelites were commanded to worship God and God alone, since they were His chosen people. Idol worship merited extermination. God spared the Israelites so that His name might not be profaned. God, the all-powerful protector, would be honored by the Gentiles.

The sins of the first generation in the desert were rebellion and apostasy in the wilderness (Ezekiel 20:8–17). The second generation committed the same sins as their fathers in the desert, and even more grievous sins. They sinned in spite of warnings; yet God did not annihilate them for His name's sake. The death-dealing ordinances of Ezekiel 20:25 may refer to Canaanite observances like the sacrifice of the firstborn to Moloch. Israel experienced the seductions of pagan worship. Yet, God's holiness guaranteed that anything coming from Him must be objectively good for His people. His purpose was to terrify them by the enormity of their trespasses. Saint Paul teaches similarly that God allowed sin to abound that man might realize his own weakness and seek divine assistance (Romans 5–6).

Ezekiel recalls the sins in Canaan, like worship on high places, *bamah* in Hebrew, and various licentious practices. Sins committed in exile, mainly idolatry, made the deportees unworthy of hearing from the Lord. Tertullian says that the new Passover, the Eucharist, will be a critical time, since it will separate those who are to be saved from those who will fall away. But then, in Ezekiel 20:33–44, restoration is predicted. God will reassemble His chosen people from the nations, among whom they are dispersed, as in a second exodus, and will judge them. The wicked will perish and the good shall return to Palestine. *"I will make you pass under the rod, and I will let you go in by number,"* (Ezekiel 20:37) suggests the shepherd's rod, under which his sheep pass as they enter the fold at night. God will also count the number of those permitted to return.

The Sword of God against Jerusalem and Ammon—Ezekiel sees a fire consuming all the trees of Judah, a figure of the sword of the Lord massacring all the inhabitants.

Then, in verse, he describes the sword and its work of destruction. In a third scene a sword (Nebuchadnezzar) consults his oracles at the crossroads to determine whether he should first assail Jerusalem or Rabbah of the Ammonites. The oracles actually tell him to attack Jerusalem. Then Ammon's subsequent punishment is prophesied. This final invasion of Judah began in winter 598 BC.

The Southern Kingdom of Judah is portrayed like a forest about to be burned. Just as a wild fire spares no trees, so Nebuchadnezzar will not spare any person, just or unjust. This prophecy of indiscriminate slaughter by a human agent does not contradict Ezekiel's teaching on man's individual accountability before God. His symbolic act of groaning foretells the sapping of men's faculties and strength in the face of such great tribulation.

"You have despised the rod, my son" (Ezekiel 21:10), seems to indicate Zedekiah despising all authority, even that of Nebuchadnezzar. God then orders Ezekiel to make a graphic representation of the two possible roads open to the Babylonian invader. The king decides, through divination, to march on Jerusalem, sealing the guilt of that city for having violated the oath of allegiance to Nebuchadnezzar. Having smitten Jerusalem, the fateful sword will turn against Ammon.

The crimes of Jerusalem (Ezekiel 22)—First, there is a list of various offenses of the citizens. Jerusalem, filled with fugitives during the siege, is then likened to a melting pot used for base metals. Finally, the sins of various classes are recorded: princes, priests, high officials, prophets, and common people, to prove that all are at fault. Ezekiel shows idolatry and bloodshed as the major crimes of Jerusalem, along with many others. The figure of the melting pot appears to refer to destruction rather than testing or refining. Israel had become like dross, worthless metal to God. There is a universal state of corruption. All classes of people have sinned grievously, and there is no one to save the nation from disaster.

Infidelity and punishment of Samaria and Jerusalem (Ezekiel 23)—Ezekiel employs bold imagery to develop the comparison begun in chapter 16. Samaria, standing for the larger Northern Kingdom of Israel, and Jerusalem, representing the Southern Kingdom are two sisters espoused to God, but unfaithful to Him. The elder sister Samaria has already suffered for her infidelity at the hands of her paramour Assyria. How inevitable then is the catastrophe of the far more unfaithful sister Jerusalem, by Babylon her lover!

The sisters are accused of infidelity in the form of idol worship in Egypt. The names here are symbolical. Oholah (Samaria) is usually interpreted as "her own tent," while Oholibah (Jerusalem) means "my tent in her." The former may refer to the schismatic temple and worship in Samaria, contrasted with the legitimate temple in Jerusalem. Samaria's unfaithfulness and ruin are depicted when she allied herself with Assyria under Jehu in 841 BC, and more permanently under Menahem in 738 BC. Foreign alliances introduced foreign worship. Her revolt from Assyria and alliance with Egypt led to her destruction in 721 BC.

Instead of learning from her sister's doom, Jerusalem acted even more shamefully with the Assyrians, Babylonians, and Egyptians. Ahaz introduced the alliance with Assyria. Hezekiah consorted with Egypt. The paramour Babylon, formerly loved but now disdained, will be God's tool in inflicting a most terrible punishment. *"They shall cut off your nose,"* (Ezekiel 23:25) mentions an Egyptian penalty for adultery: mutilating the nose of the adulterer.

Announcement of the siege and capture of Jerusalem—Two symbolic actions connote the siege. A cauldron filled with choice meats represents the principal citizens to be cooked by fire. Fire is then applied to the empty cauldron to remove the rust, which defiles it, a sign of utter destruction. Ezekiel's wife dies suddenly on the day the siege begins. His omission of the usual mourning rites signals the attitude recommended to the exiles on learning of the city's demise.

The date of the siege must have been revealed to Ezekiel. It was the 10th of Tebet (December, January) in the 9th year of Zedekiah, 589 BC. Later the Jews marked the anniversary by a solemn fast (Zechariah 8:19). During the siege, the uncovered blood of the innocent slain in Jerusalem cries for vengeance (Leviticus 17:13), as did the blood of Abel (Genesis 4:10). While the cauldron of the city, Jerusalem, defies all attempts to purify it, it must be entirely destroyed. Furthermore, the unlamented death of Ezekiel's wife becomes a prophetic sign to the exiles. Just as he is forbidden to mourn her death publicly, so they are forbidden to deplore the devastation of Jerusalem. The public rites of mourning were baring the head and feet, veiling the lower part of the face, and partaking of a special mourning meal. Also, the restrictions imposed on Ezekiel's prophetic ministry shall cease when a fugitive from Jerusalem reports that the city has fallen.

These punishments and devastation may be difficult for contemporary readers to fathom. It is never pleasant to read about sin, rebellion, apostasy, and the subsequent punishments and chastisements that inevitably will follow. In any event, the Sacred Scriptures are divinely inspired and the entirety of the Bible is useful for transformation in grace, if read with a humble and docile spirit.

If I only read the Bible in order to see what horrible bits I can find in it, or to count up the bloodthirsty bits, then of course it won't heal me.

For one thing, the Bible reflects a certain history, but it is also a kind of path that leads us in a quite personal way and sets us in the right light. If, therefore, I read the Bible in the spirit in which it was written, from Christ, in fact, or if I read it as a believing Jew, if I read it from the right starting point, that is, and read in faith, then indeed it has the power to transform me. It leads me into the attitude of Christ; it interprets my life to me and changes me personally.

Pope Benedict XVI [Cardinal Ratzinger], *God and the World,* (San Francisco: Ignatius Press, 2002), p. 155.

1. What was God's word to the elders of Israel? Ezekiel 20:1–8

2. List some of God's commands to His people.

Exodus 20:2–7
Leviticus 18:2–5
Deuteronomy 6:5
Ezekiel 20:18–20
CCC 2811

3. Describe the response of the people to God's commands. Ezekiel 20:8

* In what aspect of the faith do you find it most difficult to be obedient to God?

4. Why did God withhold his wrath? Ezekiel 20:9

5. Explain the significance of the Holy Name.

Ezekiel 20:9
CCC 2812

* What practical thing can you do to honor God's Holy Name?

6. What did God give to the people? What fulfills this observance?

Ezekiel 20:12
CCC 2175
CCC 2176

* How do you try to make Sunday a special day of rest and worship for the Lord?

7. Explain the hope to be found in Ezekiel 20:33–44.

8. What can you learn from the following verses?

Ezekiel 20:41	
Ephesians 5:2	
Philippians 4:18	

* What kind of fragrant, pleasing and acceptable sacrifices could you offer to God?

9. Explain the prophecy in Ezekiel 21:1–12.

10. What is the purpose of the "Song of the Sword" in Ezekiel 21:14–17?

* Can you think of a contemporary situation so offensive to God that a whole nation would deserve to be punished?

** List three contemporary practices that are abhorrent to God.

11. Do the people deserve to be punished?

Ezekiel 22:6	
Ezekiel 22:7	
Ezekiel 22:8	
Ezekiel 22:9	
Ezekiel 22:10–11	
Ezekiel 22:12	

12. What is the sin of Oholah (Samaria)? Ezekiel 23:1–10

13. What is the sin of Oholibah (Jerusalem)? Ezekiel 23:11–35

14. What abomination is described in Ezekiel 23:38–39?

15. What will be the result of God's punishment? Ezekiel 23:48–49

16. How is God's covenant with Israel compared to faithful marital love?

Song of Songs 8:6–7
Tobit 8:5–8
Ezekiel 23:48

* What could you (married or single) do to strengthen faithful marital love today?

17. Compare the following verses:

Ezekiel 24:6–9
Nahum 3:1–3
Habakkuk 2:12–13

18. Why is God punishing? Ezekiel 24:12–14

19. What sorrow does Ezekiel endure? Ezekiel 24:15–24

20. What will happen to Ezekiel on the day of destruction? Ezekiel 24:27

Chapter 5

Prophecies against Nations
Ezekiel 25–32

"For thus says the Lord *God:*
Because you have clapped your hands and stamped your feet
and rejoiced with all the malice within you against the land of Israel,
therefore, behold, I have stretched out my hand against you,
and will hand you over as spoil to the nations;
and I will cut you off from the peoples and will make you perish out of the countries;
I will destroy you. Then you will know that I am the Lord.*"*
Ezekiel 25:6–7

Prophecies against Ammon, Moab, Edom and Philistia (Ezekiel 25:1–17)—Like Isaiah and Jeremiah, Ezekiel too predicts God's judgment on the Gentile nations: Ammonites, Moabites, Edomites, Philistines, Phoenicians and Egyptians. He does not denounce their idol worship but their malevolent attitude toward the Lord's sanctuary and people, because their hostility is the chief obstacle to a messianic restoration.

Ammon's sin was hostility to the temple, land and people of God; therefore, the Ammonites will disappear, and their land will become a camping-ground for desert dwellers, their Eastern neighbors. That same fate will be shared by the Moabites, and all of Moab will be exposed to invasion. Edom, descending from Esau, had long been hostile to the Israelites, and even participated actively in the overthrow of Jerusalem (Obadiah 11–14). It will have its judgment executed by the Jews themselves. In fact, it was made a vassal during the Maccabean period. God Himself will punish the Philistines, by ravaging their whole seacoast.

First prophecy against Tyre: its sin and punishment (Ezekiel 26:1–21)—Tyre was the richest and most powerful of the Phoenician cities. Built on an island off the northern coast of Palestine, it was impregnable so long as the Tyrians retained command of the sea. It had dependant cities and considerable territory on the mainland. Though they had sided with Zedekiah in his revolt against Nebuchadnezzar, they nevertheless rejoiced at the fall of Jerusalem, their commercial rival, whose trade they hoped to inherit. The demise of Tyre is attributed to God without mention of human agents. Historically, the ruin came about gradually: attacked and besieged by Nebuchadnezzar (586–574 BC), captured by Alexander the Great (332 BC), its final end came at the hands of the Saracens in 1291 AD. Ezekiel makes use of conventional language in his eschatological prophecy, and mentions *"those who descend into the Pit"* (Ezekiel 26:20): the abode of all the dead in the netherworld, usually called Sheol, here conceived as a cave of darkness.

Second prophecy against Tyre: lament for Tyre (Ezekiel 27:1–36)—The city here is likened to a magnificent ship whose construction and destruction are described in elegiac verse, that is, in the form of a lament. Ezekiel describes the building of the ship; and then highlights the commercial transactions of Tyre with a number of nations. In Ezekiel 27:25b the ship goes down with its entire crew and cargo, while other crews leave their ships in mourning, and intone a lament for Tyre. The Mediterranean peoples are stupefied, their kings are terrified, but rival trading nations hiss at Tyre in derision, rejoicing in its misfortune.

Third prophecy against Tyre: sin and punishment of the prince (Ezekiel 28:1–26)—The prince of Tyre represents wickedness and corruption, and the ongoing conflict between good and evil. The lament here, followed by a short oracle on Sidon, then predicts the restoration of Judah. The prince is seen as an embodiment of the state (see Isaiah 14:4–23). In his pride he thought himself a god, "wiser than Daniel." His death, however, will show that he is but a man, not a god. Eventually, his death without a funeral will be considered a great calamity. This section has more points of contact with Genesis 2–3 than with any other biblical passage: a description of the prince as Adam in Eden before the fall. The list of precious stones is reminiscent of Exodus 28:17–20. The general sense here seems to be that Tyre's fall from perfection will be similar to the fall in Paradise; the prince was blameless until he sinned through wrongful trade. Great trade brought riches, wealth produced pride, and pride the loss of wisdom, the folly of sin. Furthermore, Ezekiel briefly predicts the punishment of Sidon, mother city of the Phoenicians, through pestilence and the sword. The removal of Israel's enemies is the prelude to the restoration, in which God will manifest His sanctity to the Gentiles.

First prophecy against Egypt: ruin and restoration (Ezekiel 29:1–16)—The pride of the Pharaoh, who is compared to a mighty crocodile, shall be humbled. Egypt which proved to be an unreliable support for Israel, shall first be devastated and then restored, but not to her former greatness. Again, Pharaoh is described as a great crocodile wallowing complacently in the security and richness of the Nile and its streams before being brought down, caught by a fisherman's hook. He and his satellites will be removed from their natural element and cast into the desert unburied, a prey for birds and beasts. Egypt is denounced as a weak and unstable ally, like a reed staff, which suddenly breaks, piercing the hand of its user or harming him through a fall. In point of fact, Egypt had sent only token help to Judah (Jeremiah 37:5–7). In the future it will be restored to a minor power, unable to deceive Israel by an alliance, serving to remind Israel of its own iniquity. Historically, the Persian Cambyses overcame Egypt and incorporated it into the Persian empire (529–522 BC).

Second prophecy against Egypt: conquest of Nebuchadnezzar (Ezekiel 29:17–21)—This is the latest of Ezekiel's dated prophecies, March 571 BC. Nebuchadnezzar, servant of God, is to be given the land of Egypt as payment for his unrequited labors in the long and arduous siege of Tyre. The riches of Tyre, which had been exhausted, will be compensated by the riches of Egypt. The horn is a biblical symbol of strength and appears frequently in messianic contexts. At any rate, the Babylonian conquest of Egypt in 568 BC made the prophet's co-exiles more ready to accept his teaching.

Third prophecy against Egypt: the day of the Lord (Ezekiel 30:1–19)—This undated prophecy portrays the fate of Egypt on the day of judgment for all nations. *"Wail, 'Alas for the day!' For the day is near, the day of the LORD is near; it will be a day of clouds, a time of doom for the nations"* (Ezekiel 30:2–3). Compare this verse with similar warnings expressed by the Prophet Isaiah. *"Wail, for the day of the LORD is near"* (Isaiah 13:6). *"Behold, the day of the LORD comes, cruel, with wrath and fierce anger, to make the earth a desolation and to destroy its sinners from it"* (Isaiah 13:9).

Fourth prophecy against Egypt: breaking of Pharaoh's arm, (Ezekiel 30:20–26)—The might of Egypt will diminish, that of Babylon increase, symbolized by broken and strengthened arms respectively. In fact, Egypt's Pharaoh before Babylonia's Nebuchadnezzar appears like a man mortally wounded. *"Therefore thus says the Lord GOD: Behold, I am against Pharaoh king of Egypt, and will break his arms, both the strong arm and the one that was broken; and I will make the sword fall from his hand"* (Ezekiel 30:22).

Fifth prophecy against Egypt: the cedar is felled (Ezekiel 31:1–18)—This prophecy in poetic form is dated May 587 BC. Using images that occur elsewhere in the Old Testament, Ezekiel compares Egypt to a magnificent cedar which is now laid low. Tree symbolism is among the most ancient biblical figures for the kingdom of God as illustrated by the tree of knowledge and the tree of life in the Garden of Eden, (Genesis 2:17; 3:22). But when he declares that even those trees in the Garden of Eden could not rival this cedar, then we have an element of biblical hyperbole, or exaggeration, here, in that Babylonia and Assyria at an earlier date were more powerful than Egypt. The prophet then employs the "taunt-song" made famous by Isaiah 13–14. The felling of the cedar, representing Pharaoh's pride, brings ruin also to the nations who depended on him, and who perish with him. While the people on earth quake at his fall and nature mourns, those already in Sheol (*"the pit"*) are consoled to know that now the high and mighty Pharaoh has sunk to their level (Isaiah 14:8–15). Moreover, Pharaoh's association with those slain by the sword implies privation of burial rites.

Sixth prophecy against Egypt: lament for Pharaoh (Ezekiel 32:1–16)—Pharaoh, representing all of Egypt, is likened to a crocodile. The sense seems to be that while he considered himself a roaring lion among the nations, in reality he was but a crocodile limited to its own environment, and when removed from that habitat it becomes the prey of birds and beasts. Ezekiel passes easily from this figure to the reality, the Egyptians. Also, the cosmic disturbances associated with the Day of Judgment underscore the magnitude of the catastrophe. The utter desolation of the land causes consternation in other nations. Some mourn, others shiver in anticipation and fear of like punishment at Babylon's hands.

Seventh and last prophecy against Egypt: Pharaoh in Sheol (Ezekiel 32:17–32)— We may date this prophecy six weeks after the preceding one. It describes Pharaoh's descent to the netherworld and his condition there. Noteworthy is the distinction of two classes in Sheol: the heroes of old have a privileged position in the upper part of the underworld (Psalm 49:15), whereas the uncircumcised and those slain in battle occupy a lower level in the Pit. With these latter are associated the Egyptians and other belligerent nations, oppressors of weaker people. No mention is made of Israel here. Assyria, first of the powerful but proud nations, finds itself in disgrace at the bottom of the Pit. Likewise, the once mighty Elam, which had extended from the Persian Gulf to Assyria, suffers the same fate. The selected list of those in Sheol is completed with mention of Edom, the princes of the north, possibly Syrians, and the Sidonians. Lastly, Pharaoh will find some measure of comfort in finding that these other oppressors share his disgrace.

Although it may seem in these sections of Sacred Scripture that God is very vengeful and punishing, it is good to remember that God is all just and all merciful. While God longs for the sinner to repent, He cannot stay His hand forever. Ultimately, if an individual or a nation refuses to appropriate the grace given for redemption and restoration, it will place itself in the path of God's righteous judgment and deserved punishment.

> God never deserts a man, unless first He is deserted by that man. For even if a man shall have committed grievous sins, once, and twice, and a third time, God still looks for him, just as He says through the Prophet, *"So that he may be converted and live"* (Ezekiel 33:11). But if a man begins to continue in his sins, despair is born of the multitude of those sins, and obduracy is begotten of despair … Obduracy is not effected by the compelling power of God, but is gotten of the forgiveness and indulgence of God. And thus, it must be believed that it was not divine power, but divine patience that hardened [hearts].
>
> (Saint Caesar of Arles [470–542 AD], *Sermons*, 101. 22, 2)

1. Why was God displeased with the Ammonites? Ezekiel 25:1–7

2. How would Moab be punished? Ezekiel 25:8–11

3. What can you learn from the following verses?

Ezekiel 25:12–14
Leviticus 19:18
Deuteronomy 32:35

4. What should be done instead of vengeance or hatred? Matthew 5:44

* Have you ever tried following Matthew 5:44 when you wanted to get revenge?

5. Compare the following verses:

Isaiah 14:29–31
Jeremiah 47:1–7
Ezekiel 25:15–17

6. What destruction is prophesied against Tyre? Ezekiel 26:1–21

7. Describe the ending of the Lamentation over Tyre. Ezekiel 27:32–36

8. What is foretold in Ezekiel 28:1–10?

9. Who is lamented in Ezekiel 28:11–19?

10. Explain the prophecy against Sidon. Ezekiel 28:20–23

11. Find the hope in Ezekiel 28:25–26.

* What is the basis of our hope? Colossians 1:27

** Are you generally hopeful or fearful? How can you demonstrate hope?

12. Explain the prophecy in Ezekiel 29:1–16.

13. What will happen according to Ezekiel 29:17–21?

14. Compare the following verses:

Isaiah 13:6–9
Ezekiel 30:1–9

15. What physical injury represents the fall of Pharaoh? Ezekiel 30:20–26

16. What imagery is used to represent Pharaoh in Ezekiel 31:1–9?

* What contemporary power could you compare to Pharaoh?

17. What will happen to Pharaoh and why? Ezekiel 31:10–18

18. What lament is made over Pharaoh? Ezekiel 32:1–16

* How do you think people suffer because of the sins of their leaders?

19. Explain the place described in these verses:

Ezekiel 32:17–32
CCC 633

20. What sin may have caused Pharaoh's fall?

Proverbs 16:18
CCC 1866

* What is a practical antidote to the sin of pride?

Chapter 6

Salvation for Israel
Ezekiel 33–39

"A new heart I will give you, and a new spirit I will put within you;
and I will take out of your flesh the heart of stone and give you a heart of flesh.
And I will put my spirit within you, and cause you to walk in my statutes
and be careful to observe my ordinances.
You shall dwell in the land which I gave to your fathers;
and you shall be my people, and I will be your God."
Ezekiel 36:26–28

Conditions of salvation (Ezekiel 33:1–33)—Here Ezekiel addresses the purification and restoration of Israel. Chapter 33 introduces the third part of the book of the prophet Ezekiel. In some ways it repeats and develops four instructions already given. The first and second parts treat of the prophet's functions and personal responsibility; the third and fourth are admonitions addressed respectively to the Israelites in Palestine who were not deported, and to Ezekiel's companions in exile. The occasion of the prophecy was the arrival of a fugitive with news of Jerusalem's capture, narrated in the third section. A prophet is like a watchman who is obliged to be on the alert and to give warning of an enemy's approach. If, therefore, the prophet gives due warning, the sinner alone is responsible for what happens. If the prophet fails to warn, however, he too is held accountable.

Ezekiel reminds the hearer of his personal responsibility. Punishment of the nation for sins in which the exiles participated causes the latter to despair of pardon, but the prophet reminds them of God's justice and mercy. He will not blame them for the sins of others, and is always ready to pardon repentant sinners. At the same time, the righteous person must persevere in justice, just as the sinner must repair the wrong he has done. And indeed, God's ways are eternally just and thus forbid despair: repentance of evil and perseverance in good will bring salvation. Saint John of Damascene says that we should confess our sins, for God is rich in mercy.

Israelites who were not deported are then admonished. Ezekiel is told of the fall of Jerusalem, and at the same time receives full liberty of speech in preaching to the people. This news reached the exiles about six months after the city's fall. He rejects the claims of those not exiled to the possession of Palestine. Ezekiel was in an ecstasy from the evening to the following morning, when the fugitive visited him as already announced in Ezekiel 24:26. The survivors in Judah argue that the land belongs to them. Abraham as an individual possessed the land. They as his descendants are more numerous and able to populate and cultivate the land, and therefore have a stronger claim to it. The prophet, however, tells them that as sinners they are doomed to destruction. And indeed, many of them must have suffered in the subsequent deportation in 582 BC, mentioned in Jeremiah 52:30. The Lord reproaches Ezekiel's fellow-exiles for their duplicity in listening to the prophet but not really heeding his words or carrying out his instructions: *"And behold, you are to them like one who sings love songs"* (Ezekiel 33:32a). But their eyes will be opened in the day of their chastisement.

The bad shepherds replaced by a New David (Ezekiel 34:1–31)—In this important prophecy the Lord compares Israel to a flock of sheep, neglected, preyed on and dispersed by bad shepherds. He intends to purify them, to restore them to their old pasturage where they shall find abundant nourishment and where a single shepherd, called David and the servant of God, shall rule them in tranquility and holiness (Jeremiah 23:1–8). This messianic prophecy comes to its truest fulfillment in the New Testament, especially in the parables in which Jesus Christ likens His own work to a shepherd; it culminates in John 10:11: *"I am the Good Shepherd."*

The unworthy shepherds—kings, priests and prophets of old—took full remunerations for duties, which they did not perform. These bad individuals did not assist the weak, the sick, the wounded and strayed, who needed their ministrations. Instead they ruled the flock harshly. The wild beasts—symbolic of foreign nations—would attack and disperse the flock. And so, the bad leaders will be called to account and will be deprived of their office. Ezekiel 34:11–16 illustrates God as the Good Shepherd of His flock. As part of Israel's restoration and salvation the Lord Himself will pasture the flock (see also Isaiah 40:11; Psalm 23). As a shepherd reunites his scattered sheep, so shall God reunite His scattered people. He will do all that the evil shepherds failed to do.

The Hebrew word for flock, *eder,* includes goats as well as sheep. Rams and he-goats in particular indicate the ruling classes inclined to selfishness. The stronger animals, having satisfied themselves, trample the pasture and foul the waters. The fat are the oppressors, the lean the oppressed. Divine judgment will imply removal of disturbances from the flock. The messianic kingdom is often represented as a revival of David's reign. The Messiah is a New David, servant of God. His rule will be peaceful and prosperous: the New Covenant is a Covenant of peace. That in the same context God Himself and the New David (Messiah) are said to shepherd Israel apparently did not have any fuller significance for Ezekiel. Only later, Jesus, as the Son of God and Son of Man, was to apply the prophecy to Himself.

Devastation of Edom (Ezekiel 35:1–15)—The prophets depict the messianic restoration as the reestablishment of Israel in all her ancestral territory. After the fall of Jerusalem, Edom had occupied a considerable part of Judah and aspired to possession of all Israel, which ultimately belongs to God. The punishment of unbrotherly Edom, already announced in Ezekiel 25:12–14, is again predicted here as an integral part of the program of restoration. Incidentally, "Seir" refers to the mountainous region of Edom. Its offense is perpetual enmity towards Judah, manifested particularly in the recent calamity either by their slaying of Israelite fugitives or by handing them over to the Chaldeans: *"blood shall pursue you; because you are guilty of blood!"* (Ezekiel 35:6). In this verse there is a play on words. "Dam" in Hebrew is contained in the name Edom.

Reestablishment of Israel (Ezekiel 36:1–38)—The Gentiles attributed Israel's degradation to the weakness of the Lord, her protector and mentor. Hence Israel must be reestablished so that God's name be no longer blasphemed; the devastated land will increase in fertility and the sinful people will be spiritually regenerated. The prophecy is conditional, however, and depends for its literal fulfillment on the cooperation of Israel with the designs of God. It was eventually fulfilled in the spiritual Israel, the Catholic Church, founded by Christ. It is not for Israel's sake that the renewal takes place, nor due to her merits. Rather, the Lord's holy name should no longer be blasphemed by the Gentiles, who thought Him unable to protect His chosen people. The prediction includes the return of the deportees to Palestine. *"I will sprinkle clean water upon you, and you shall be clean from all your uncleannesses ... A new heart I will give you, and a new spirit I will put within you"* (Ezekiel 36:25) suggests a baptismal regeneration through the image of washing with water and the infusion of God's spirit. The prophetic text also stresses the necessity for repentance for past transgressions. Then neighboring nations will recognize the hand of the Lord and no longer mock His holy name, while He will multiply His people. The comparison with sheep suggests the numerous flocks assembled at the solemn feast in Jerusalem.

The vision of the dry bones restored to life (Ezekiel 37:1–14)—This amazing vision refers to the revival of the defunct nation of Israel, hopelessly scattered in exile. Saint Ambrose believes that this vision foretells the resurrection of the body, in that it reverses the order of nature, and providentially prepares for later revelation on the resurrection of the dead and future judgment. The scene of the vision was a plain near Tel-abib mentioned in Ezekiel 3:22. The dry bones symbolize the house of Israel as politically not existent. The graves were the places where dispersed Israelites lived as strangers in foreign lands, waiting for their deliverance and return to their own land causing a national renaissance.

The symbolic action of joining together two sticks signifies the reunion of the divided kingdoms of Judah and Israel by God's will; they shall form a single nation under a single ruler, the New David, in their ancestral territory. God will make an eternal alliance with them and set up His sanctuary within them. This prophecy is clearly messianic and spiritually fulfilled in the one true Church, the Catholic Church. Judah and Joseph, whose names are written on the sticks, were the tribal ancestors whose descendants played the leading roles in the kingdoms of Judah and Israel, and the division which had historically separated Israelite from Israelite shall be no more. The deportees will return and form a new reign, and the New David—Jesus the Messiah—shall rule over them forever, and from the sanctuary in their midst—perhaps allusive of His Real Presence in the Eucharist—He shall become known to the Gentiles. Notice that, unlike Isaiah, Ezekiel never depicts the Messiah except as a New David. Saint Jerome saw the life-giving Spirit in the dry bones similar to the life-giving Spirit shared in the Eucharist.

Final victory of the Lord over the pagan world (Ezekiel 38–39)—While Israel enjoys peace and prosperity in her native land after the restoration, Gog, ruler of the northern nations, leads a mighty army against her. Yet God protects His people by annihilating the inimical forces as they reach Palestine. We find a description of the burning of weapons, the burial of the slain, and the feasting of predatory birds and beasts. Ezekiel's main goal is to assure his audience of the Lord's permanent protection. The literary genre employed is apocalyptic, shot through with symbolism. Thus, the meaning may be literally historical, as well as messianic (Revelation 20:7) and eschatological. Eschatological means relating to the end-time that falls together with the first coming of Christ and including the entire history of the Church. Those who understand this prophecy in a literal, that is, historical sense attempt to identify Gog with some specific foreign invader, the Seleucids for instance. Others, who see a messianic meaning, explain Gog and his army as signaling the forces of evil seeking vainly to undermine the Church founded on the Rock, which is Christ. Again other commentators take it as an eschatological passage, that is, as the struggle between the forces of good and evil, which will precede the last judgment.

Gog's invasion of Israel (Ezekiel 38:1–23)—There is a portrayal of Gog's army, his scheming against Israel, and finally his defeat by God. The line-up of armies emphasizes the sheer ferocity and power aligned against God's covenanted people. The nations mentioned indicate all the might of paganism, drawn from the far reaches of the earth. These kingdoms of the world rise against the kingdom of God, symbolized in restored Israel, but their attack is doomed to failure. An invasion of Israel was traditionally expected to come from the north. Nevertheless, the actual meaning or derivation of the names of "Gog" and "Magog" is not certain. The name Gog has been linked with Agag (1 Samuel 15:8–33), with Gyges the king of Lydia, and with various other historical persons, whereas Magog appears in Genesis 10:2. In the messianic and eschatological interpretation of this text, "Gog and Magog" symbolizes all the forces of evil ranged against God's people, a sort of Antichrist. In the Apocalypse of Saint John (Revelation 20:8ff), Magog becomes an independent figure at the side of Gog; both are kings summoned by evil spirits at the end of the millennium to fight against God's people, only to suffer utter destruction by fire from heaven. The Gog occurrences in Ezekiel profoundly influenced later apocalyptic literature on a whole.

Gog's design is to plunder a peaceful and naturally unprotected people, Israel, "who dwell at the navel [center] of the earth" (Ezekiel 38:12). It was not unknown for ancient peoples to refer to their own homeland as the navel of the earth. Also, the inquiries of the trading nations are explained by the fact that traders attended armies to purchase the pillage, including slaves (1 Maccabees 3:41; 2 Maccabees 8:10). But then God Himself annihilates the enemy, revealing Himself as in a theophany: the earth trembles, birds and fishes, men and animals are terrified, mountains are overturned, rocks are rent and walls collapse. The enemies end up slaying their own men (2 Chronicles 20:23), or are slain by the angel of the Lord (2 Kings 19:35), by hailstones (Joshua 10:11), or by lightning (Genesis 19:24).

Sequel to the victory (Ezekiel 39:1–24)—A recapitulation of the preceding prophecy stresses the total demise of the invaders from the north. Gog's own land will suffer, as well as the coastlands of his allies. The burning of weapons and burial of the casualties is pictured in Ezekiel 39:9–16: uninterrupted peace following the victory makes weapons useless, and indicates that this would be the last attempt to wage war against Israel. It would take seven months just to bury all the remains and so purify the land. Indeed the victims resemble a sacrificial feast prepared by the Lord. Their corpses are so numerous that before they can be buried many will serve as food for carrion birds and animals. Finally, as with Antichrist, so with Gog and Magog, there have been numerous attempts to identify them with individual persecutors in the course of history. Ezekiel 39:25–28 offers a summary conclusion of the restoration prophecies: the return of the exiles, their spiritual rebirth, and God's abiding presence among them, all glorify His name.

1. Compare the duties of a watchman with the results.

	Duty	Result
Exekiel 33:1–5		
Ezekiel 33:6–7		
Ezekiel 33:8		
Ezekiel 33:9		
Ezekiel 33:13		
Ezekiel 33:14–16		

* Have you ever felt God nudging you to confront someone who was wandering?

** Were you obedient to God? What was the result?

2. What does God desire?

Ezekiel 33:11
Hosea 14:1–4
1 Timothy 2:3–4

3. What happened in Ezekiel 33:21–22?

4. Why does God punish the people? Ezekiel 33:25–29

5. Write the main idea of these passages in one sentence.

Jeremiah 23:1–4
Ezekiel 34:1–16
John 10:11–15
1 Peter 5:4

6. Explain the sheepfold.

Ezekiel 34:11–31
CCC 754

7. Explain the prophecy against Mount Seir. Ezekiel 35:1–15

8. Through whom can you find a hope of salvation?

Ezekiel 36:1–15
CCC 64

9. Explain the importance of the Holy Name of God.

Ezekiel 36:20–22
CCC 2814

10. What sacrament is foreshadowed in this passage?

Ezekiel 36:25
CCC 1214
CCC 1215

* One way to be made clean from all uncleanness is to celebrate the Sacrament of Reconciliation. When is this Sacrament offered in your parish? How often do you celebrate the Sacrament of Reconciliation and receive these graces?

11. What can you learn about the heart from these passages?

Psalm 51:10–12
Ezekiel 36:25–28
CCC 368
CCC 715

* Do you have a heart of stone (a hard heart) or a heart of flesh (a soft heart)?

12. What is needed to animate the dry bones?

Ezekiel 37:1–14
CCC 703

* Share some ways in which you can become animated when you feel dry.

13. Who do the two sticks represent in Ezekiel 37:15–24?

14. Describe the New Covenant that God will make. Ezekiel 37:24–28

15. Are "Gog and Magog" good guys or bad guys? Ezekiel 38:1–23

* List some of the bad guys in contemporary history.

16. Compare these verses:

Ezekiel 38:22	
Revelation 8:7	

17. What will ultimately happen to Gog and Magog? Ezekiel 39:1–20

18. What will God do according to Ezekiel 39:21–24?

19. What characteristic of God can you find in these verses?

Psalm 69:16	
Ezekiel 39:25	

20. What does God promise in Ezekiel 39:29? Ask God for more of the Holy Spirit.

Monthly Social Activity

This month, your small group will meet for coffee, tea, or a simple breakfast, lunch, or dessert in someone's home. Pray for this social event and for the host or hostess. Try, if at all possible, to attend.

After a short prayer and some time for small talk, write a few sentences about a time in your life when you felt that God had given you a new heart, or given you refreshment in the Holy Spirit. Make sure that everyone has time to share.

Examples

◆ *I went to Confession after a very long time and felt a lightness of spirit, as if I were home again.*

◆ *After lots of prayer and counsel with a priest, I was finally able to forgive someone who had betrayed me.*

◆ *Once on a retreat, I felt a fresh outpouring of the Holy Spirit on me.*

Chapter 7

The New Israel
Ezekiel 40–48

*As the glory of the LORD entered the temple by the gate facing east,
the Spirit lifted me up, and brought me into the inner court;
and behold, the glory of the LORD filled the temple.*
Ezekiel 43:4–5

The final prediction of the restoration (Ezekiel 40–48)—In this last section of the book, Ezekiel concludes his prophecies on the restoration with a detailed and magnificent description of the New Temple, the New Cult, and the New Promised and Holy Land. Catholic tradition has usually regarded this picture as a prefiguring of the messianic kingdom, the Church founded by Christ. Saint Gregory the Great saw the city as the Church. Saint Jerome saw God as the Master-builder and the life of the Gospel lying before those who enter the temple precincts. On a technical plane, the text transmission of these chapters is rather faulty, often corrupt and unintelligible, and so a few details are necessarily conjectural.

The New Temple (Ezekiel 40–42)—Ezekiel is transported in spirit to Jerusalem and ordered to communicate to the house of Israel what is there revealed to him. The approximate date is 10th Nisan (March-April) 573 BC. From a high mountain the prophet sees the temple (Ezekiel 40:2; Revelation 21:10). A resplendent angel in human form guides the prophet and takes various measures with a reed or cord. In the process the east gate is described as being the most important though similar to the north and south gates. Ezekiel 40:28–47 presents the inner court and its gates, all inspected by the prophet. This temple, like Solomon's, had four parts: Vestibule, Holy Place, Holy of Holies, and Lateral Building. Entering into those spaces may be compared to that of the high priest on the Day of Atonement (Leviticus 16). The entrances to each part of the temple are progressively narrower as one reaches a precinct of greater sacredness. Ezekiel's illustrations are completed with the buildings of the inner court and sanctuary proper.

The New Cult (Ezekiel 43–46)—God now enters His temple and prescribes how He is to be worshipped there. Ezekiel beholds the glory of the Lord (theophany) and hears His voice. God will dwell forever among His people; they shall no more profane His holy name by their infidelities. He orders the prophet to promulgate the plan and measurements of the New Temple together with the laws regulating temple service now being revealed to him. After describing the altar of holocausts and its consecration, the prophet mentions those admitted to the temple. The closed gate, through which God alone has passed, has been understood by many Fathers of the Church as a figure of Our Lady's perpetual virginity. Furthermore, the prince in Ezekiel 44:3 is the vice-regent of God who is king of the new theocratic state. Among His privileges is a special place for sacrificial meals at the east gate.

"And he said to me, 'This gate shall remain shut; it shall not be opened, and no one shall enter by it; for the LORD, the God of Israel, has entered by it; therefore it shall remain shut'" (Ezekiel 44:2).

> Who is this gate, if not Mary? Is it not closed because she is a virgin? Mary is the gate through which Christ entered this world, when He was brought forth in the virginal birth and the manner of His birth did not break the seals of virginity.
>
> (Saint Ambrose of Milan [333–397 AD], *The Consecration of a Virgin and the Perpetual Virginity of Mary*, 8, 52)

Ezekiel reproaches the Israelites for having permitted foreigners and uncircumcised persons, whom they employed in an inferior capacity as temple servants, to enter and profane the Lord's sanctuary. They must be replaced by those Levites who at one time exercised sacerdotal functions but who had been degraded by their idol worship and infidelity to God. Another eloquent detail is that the priests are no longer all the male descendants of Aaron in general, but the descendants of Zadok in particular: Abiathar, the high priest in David's time, was descended from Aaron's son Ithamar. His disloyalty led to a transfer of the priestly dignity to the loyal Zadok, a descendant of Aaron's other son Eleazar (1 Kings 1:26–35). Thus, the faithfulness of Zadok and his lineage in the service of the Lord at a time of general apostasy motivates their choice as priests in the New Temple.

Ezekiel 45:1–17 reports on the allotment of land to the priests and to the prince. The prince's portion extends vastly to the Mediterranean on the West and to the Dead Sea on the East. This ample provision for the prince seems to be designed to correct an ancient abuse by which monarchs arbitrarily appropriated tribal territory. Then, feasts and sacrifices are addressed. Two feasts of expiation seem to replace the one Day of Atonement (*Yom Kippur*). Surprisingly, there is no mention of pivotal Old Testament realities such as the paschal lamb, of first-fruits and of the feast of Pentecost. Ezekiel 46:16–18 shows the inalienability of the prince's domain: only to his sons can he make a permanent gift of part of his domain.

The New Holy Land (Ezekiel 47–48)—The prophet first outlines the temple river, then the boundaries of the land, and lastly the distribution of it. Water, especially in the dry countries of the east, is a familiar symbol of abundance and life, whether of earthly or spiritual nature (John 4:14; 7:38). Yet it may also mean punishment (Isaiah 8:5–8). The symbol is not confined to Israelite tradition. Saint Jerome saw the waters flowing from the temple as representing the teaching of the Church. Barnabas saw the waters of baptism overflowing with spiritual nourishment. Now, so powerful are the life-giving waters of the river issuing from the temple that they even transform the Dead Sea into a fresh-water lake teeming with fish. A vivid vignette shows the fishermen drying their nets by it (Ezekiel 47:10). Ezekiel 47:13–23 considers the limits of David's realm (2 Samuel 8:3–12; 2 Kings 14:25).

The presence of the Lord in His temple, indicated by the river, which flows from there, may be compared with the glory of God in Ezekiel 9:3. There the Almighty passed judgment on a wicked generation: here in the new age He dispenses benefits to a chastised and repentant nation. They are envisaged as dwelling in peace within their restored borders in a prosperous and fertile land. Nature itself will partake of God's blessing. Ezekiel, when explaining the distribution of tribal portions (Ezekiel 48:1–35), begins by giving foreigners in the Holy Land a share in its territory (Psalm 87), and thus the distinction between Jew and Gentile tends to disappear in the messianic kingdom. He then assigns a strip of land to each of the twelve tribes, albeit Levi receives no portion among them.

Overall, the reconstitution, which Ezekiel contemplates, is not so much practical as it is ideal and messianic. Interestingly, the post-exilic re-builders of Solomon's temple in the 5th century BC, guided by prophets and priests, made no effort to realize the prophet Ezekiel's blueprint. His legislation, which ignored the high priest and was sometimes at variance with the mosaic code, was never really accepted as authoritative. In his description of the Holy Land there are several features, especially the temple river, that defy a realistic interpretation, and therefore invite a mystical interpretation in the guise of Isaiah's vision of the New Jerusalem. Finally, bringing together the message of the entire prophecy, the name of the New City will be *"The Lord is there!"* (Ezekiel 48:35).

1. Describe some aspects of the new temple.

Ezekiel 40:6–19
Ezekiel 40:20–27
Ezekiel 40:28–37
Ezekiel 40:38–47
Ezekiel 41:1–15
Ezekiel 42:1–20

2. Describe the vision in Ezekiel 43:1–5.

3. What must be put away for the Lord to dwell in their midst? Ezekiel 43:9

* Is there anything that the Lord is inviting you to put away or put aside for Him?

4. What can you learn from these passages?

Ezekiel 44:2
CCC 499
CCC 500
CCC 501

* What type of devotion do you have toward our Blessed Virgin Mother?

** What type of Marian devotions and sacramentals do you enjoy?

5. Who will and who will not be admitted to the temple?

Ezekiel 44:4–9
Ezekiel 44:10–14
Ezekiel 44:15–31

6. How shall the land be apportioned?

Ezekiel 45:1–4
Ezekiel 45:5–6
Ezekiel 45:7–8

7. What does the Lord demand in these verses?

Leviticus 19:15
Deuteronomy 25:13–16
Ezekiel 45:9–12
Amos 8:5

* How just are you in your dealings? Do you treat others as you would be treated? Or do you try to get the better of the deal for yourself without respect for others?

8. What offerings does God request?

Ezekiel 45:13–17
Malachi 3:10–11

* Rank in order with 1 being highest. To whom are you most generous?

___ Myself

___ My loved ones

___ God

9. What feast is reflected in these verses?

Exodus 12:1–12
Ezekiel 45:18–25

10. What did Jesus institute at a later Passover?

Matthew 26:17–28
Mark 14:16–25
Luke 22:15–20

* Share about how important the Eucharist is in your life.

11. How important should the Eucharist be in the Christian life? CCC 1324

12. Compare the following verses:

Ezekiel 46:13
John 1:29
1 Peter 1:19
Revelation 5:6–12

13. What can you learn from the following verses?

Sirach 24:30–31
Ezekiel 47:1–12
Joel 3:18
Zechariah 13:1
Revelation 22:1–5

* How do you think you would react if God called you to be a prophet and asked you to wade in the water up to your waist?

14. How important is water to physical life and spiritual life?

John 6:35
Revelation 7:16–17

15. Why did God assign new boundaries to the land? Ezekiel 47:21–23

16. How was the land apportioned? Ezekiel 48:1–7

17. Who received a sacred tract? Ezekiel 48:8–14

18. Who received a portion parallel to the tribal portions? Ezekiel 48:21

19. What is the name of the city? Ezekiel 48:35

20. Ultimately, what city would you like to live in? Revelation 21:10–21

Chapter 8

Higher than Angels
Hebrews 1–2

In many and various ways God spoke of old to our fathers by the prophets;
but in these last days he has spoken to us by a Son,
whom he appointed the heir of all things, through whom also he created the world.
He reflects the glory of God and bears the very stamp of his nature,
upholding the universe by his word of power.
When he had made purification for sins,
he sat down at the right hand of the Majesty on high,
having become as much superior to angels
as the name he has obtained is more excellent than theirs.
Hebrews 1:1–4

ebrews is one of the most beautiful but controversial books in the New Testament. Neither its author nor the intended audience is named. It seems very Jewish and it was written before the destruction of the temple in AD 70. The introduction (Hebrews 1:1–4) places the coming of Jesus Christ in the context of Jewish history. This leads to a section that compares Jesus as God's Son to the angels (Hebrews 1:5–2:18). The recurring theme is that Jesus is superior to any Old Testament reality. The bulk of the letter is dedicated to a unique image found nowhere else in the New Testament, Jesus as the High Priest (Hebrews 3:1–10:39). Despite His exaltation Jesus compassionately identifies with our human condition. Paradoxically, He is at the same time Priest and Victim for our sins. The next section (Hebrews 11:1–12:29) praises the heroic faith of the Jewish ancestors. The epistle concludes with a series of exhortations to live upright lives (Hebrews 13).

In order to understand this letter one has to know many of the Old Testament figures and the nature of worship. A twofold purpose of the letter can be discerned: First, it explains in an orderly fashion the significance of Jesus Christ in comparison to the angels, Moses and Aaron. Jesus now replaces and surpasses the entire Old Testament reality. Second, it provides strong ethical encouragement to its readers to advance in the new path of Christ's Church, and not to turn back to the old ways. Hebrews has great theological importance. Its Christological doctrine, in particular, crowns the Christology of Saint Paul and advances to the very threshold of Johannine heights. God pervades the letter chiefly as the Revealer speaking formerly through the prophets and last of all through His Son. The teaching of the epistle is undoubtedly Trinitarian (Hebrews 2:3f). Christ is the center of Paul's thought; He is, above all, the Son of God and the Savior. His Lordship is recognized in the title "Our Lord" (Hebrews 7:14; 13:20). Additionally, special titles include: "Pioneer [Author] of salvation" (Hebrews 2:10), "Apostle and High Priest of our confession" (Hebrews 3:1), "Great Priest" (Hebrews 10:21), "Pioneer and perfecter of faith" (Hebrews 12:2), and "Great Shepherd of the sheep" (Hebrews 13:20). The Incarnation is set forth in an extraordinarily rich and specifically sacerdotal manner, in which the priest is the mediator between God and man. As the Author of human salvation the Son, according to a plan of solidarity with our condition, was to attain His own glory, the perfection of His Saviorship and the sympathy of His priestly quality by undergoing sufferings and death. This teaching on the Savior is called "Soteriology."

Hebrews teaches about the Holy Spirit. He is called "the Spirit of grace" and is the third Person of the Blessed Trinity. In the seven relevant texts four functions are attributed to the Holy Spirit: (1) the inspiration of Scriptures, (2) the sanctification of Christ's soul, (3) the distribution of charismata, and (4) the sanctification of the faithful. He is also the designer of the symbolical arrangements of Israelite worship (Hebrews 9:8), through Him Christ offered His eternal sacrifice (Hebrews 9:14). The faithful are not only partakers of Christ, but also partakers of the Holy Spirit.

Lastly, when closely examined Hebrews reveals an important teaching on the Church, called ecclesiology. In the first place there is every indication of a New Covenant, of which Christ is the sovereign administrator (Hebrews 2:5). The house in which Moses ministered is replaced by the house over which the Son has been placed (Hebrews 3:6). We have a common heavenly calling and hold the same confession of faith in the bond of brotherhood. Obedience to Church superiors is a sacred duty. Furthermore, the House of God also figures as a city and a kingdom, and our fellowship with heaven is realized in good measure here on earth. The Hebrew Sinai has become the Christian Zion, designating the whole Church. The myriads of angels in festive assembly, God the Judge of all, and the spirits of the just belong especially to the consummation in heaven. So, the approach to an assembly of firstborn enrolled in heaven and to the Mediator of a New Covenant and to a blood of sprinkling, which speaks better than Abel's, refers without a doubt to those who are still on the way to the final fulfillment of the promises.

Authorship—From the Early Church Fathers until today, there have been differing opinions concerning the authorship of this epistle. Saint John Chrysostom and Origen believed that Saint Paul wrote this letter personally, whereas Saint Clement of Rome and Tertullian argued that although Hebrews contains Saint Paul's thought, it was written by someone else. The Douay-Rheims Bible entitled this book "The Epistle of Saint Paul to the Hebrews," and Paul's disciple Timothy emerges in Hebrews 13:23. One reason for controversy is that the style and contents differ considerably from other Pauline letters. Also, neither the author nor intended readers are mentioned anywhere. So, we just don't know who the human author is for certain. But, since it is part of the Sacred Scriptures, we know that the Holy Spirit is the Divine Author.

The Prologue, a compendium of Christology (Hebrews 1:1–4)—Christology is that part of theology which deals with the person of our Lord Jesus Christ and His works. The customary epistolary introduction is lacking in Hebrews, and in its place stands a prologue, or foreword, which announces the themes to follow: the superiority of the New Covenant to the Old which it perfects, the divinity shared by the Son and manifested to us in Him, His preeminent place in the cosmos, His priestly character excelling Moses and Aaron in achieving salvation for us by His Passion and Transitus (passage) to the heavenly world surpassing even the angels. In order to prevent his Jewish-Christian audience in Jerusalem from falling back to Judaism, the author of Hebrews undertakes to prove Christ's transcendence over the most eminent mediators of the Old Covenant, namely the angels, Moses, and Aaron.

The multiplicity of ways in which God spoke of old is a sign of imperfection: Fathers and prophets evoke all spiritual ancestors of Israel, embracing all prophetic and historical books of the Old Testament. *"In these last days"* (Hebrews 1:2a), the fullness has arrived in the messianic Son, the one and only Word of God, ushering in the age of the Church in all its depth and breadth. Jesus is the heir of future ages in His humanity. He is the maker of the universe (in Greek *aiones* really means worlds) at the dawn of time in His divinity, combining in Himself all the functions of Wisdom (Proverbs 8:27–31; Wisdom 7:21; 9:9; Sirach 24:2–6). But the author goes beyond tradition by defining the very being of the Son in terms of a personal relationship with God, much closer than that of Wisdom. Christ is seen as the definitive consummation of creation, its Alpha (protology=the study of the origin of things; God's fundamental purpose for humanity) and Omega (eschatology=the study of the last things). Metaphorically, Jesus is the radiation of the Father's glory and the seal-imprint of His nature, expressing His divine origin and perfect unity with His Father. He also maintains and governs everything visible and invisible. *"When he had made purification for sins"* (Hebrews 1:3b) alludes to the redemption of humankind, restoring the relationship between God and His people. Thus, in this preface Jesus appears as *Prophet*, *Priest*, and *King*, sitting at God's right hand. Finally, His excellence over the angels is emphasized. For centuries this grand text has been selected for the Mass of Christmas Day.

[An angel] is called spirit and fire: spirit, as being of an intellectual nature; and fire, as being of a purifying nature ... They sing the praises of the divine majesty and contemplate eternally the eternal glory, not that God may thereby have an increase of glory, for nothing can be added to what is already full, to Him that supplies all good things to others, but that there may never be an end of blessing to those first natures after God.

(Saint Gregory Nazianzen, [330–389 AD], *Second Theological Oration*, 28, 31)

Christ transcends the angels (Hebrews 1:5–2:18)—The inferiority of the angels is proved by texts concerning them: *"All worshipers of images are put to shame, who make their boast in worthless idols; let all his angels bow down before him"* (Psalm 97:7). The Son's supremacy emerges in texts whose original literal sense applied to God, *"you are the same, and your years have no end. The children of your servants shall dwell secure; their posterity shall be established before you"* (Psalm 102:27–28) or to a messianic figure *"'I have set my king on Zion, my holy mountain.' I will tell of the decree of the*

LORD: *He said to me, 'You are my son, today I have begotten you'"*(Psalm 2:6–7; see also Psalm 45; 110). These texts come to new life if read in the light of Christ. They become conveyors of mysteries, which are now unveiled by God, who has proclaimed Jesus alone—never an angel—as His Son.

Whereas, *"You are my beloved Son; with you I am well pleased,"* (Mark 1:11) uses Psalm 2:7 for Christ's baptism, and *"This is my beloved Son; listen to him"* (Mark 9:7) the same Psalm for His Transfiguration, Hebrews highlights His glory, when Jesus in His humanity became fully head and heir of the universe. The *today* of Hebrews 1:5 can be understood as: a) the generation of the Second Divine Person from all eternity, or b) referring to His coming in the flesh as the First-born. Indeed, the First-born is also seen as returning in glory (*Parousia*=the Second Coming of Christ). Whereas the angels are like unstable elements, wind and fire, the Son is above change and forever. The quotes from a royal enthronement Psalm *"Your divine throne endures for ever and ever. Your royal scepter is a scepter of equity … Therefore God, your God, has anointed you with the oil of gladness above your fellows (Psalm 45:6–7)* are repeated in Hebrews 1:8ff to underline Jesus' permanence. His timelessness is shown under the image of a used garment.

> We believe in one God, Father almighty, Creator of all things visible and invisible; and in one Lord Jesus Christ, His Son, begotten of Him according to nature before all ages and time; for as to time He is co-unoriginate and coeternal with His own Father, seated with Him in equal honor, and enjoying equality with Him in every respect, for He is the stamp and splendor of His Substance.
>
> (Saint Cyril of Alexandria, [376–444 AD]
> *Memorials on the True Faith*, 2, 1)

"Therefore we must pay the closer attention to what we have heard, lest we drift away from it" (Hebrews 2:1) contains an exhortation based on Christ's preeminence: *what we have heard* is the proclamation (*Kerygma*) of the New Testament revelation announcing salvation in Christ and the duties incumbent on those who seek it. The reason is given in the form of an argument *a fortiori*: if the Old Testament provided for just punishment of failure to accept it, so much more will a rejection of the New Covenant bring chastisement. The idea of angels transmitting the covenant was common in first century Judaism. As Christians we have much stronger reasons for believing and putting our faith into action. *"But we see Jesus, who for a little while was made lower than the angels, crowned with glory and honor because of the suffering of death, so that by the grace of God he might taste death for every one"* (Hebrews 2:9) broaches a paradox: Jesus for a time less than the angels! Yes, in His becoming man and suffering ignominiously in an historical setting He subjected Himself temporarily, biblically speaking, to the angels. But, it is made clear that He is really concerned not with this world but with the world to come, the world of heavenly realities, already inaugurated but not completed until the parousia, the Second Coming of Jesus Christ in His glory.

"What is man that you are mindful of him, or the son of man, that you care for him? You made him for a little while lower than the angels, you have crowned him with glory and honor, putting everything in subjection under his feet" (Hebrews 2:6–8a), cites Psalm 8:5–7 in a messianic-apocalyptic sense of the Son of Man, and then gives the reader the interpretation. Although the universe is already subject to authority and dominion, but not yet totally or concretely in submission, signaling a tension between *already* and *not yet.* The actual realization of Christ's reign will happen only at the end of time. Whereas *for a little while made lower than the angels* relates to His momentary humiliation in His Passion, His being *crowned in glory,* comes true in His perpetual exaltation in His Resurrection and Ascension. Jesus' humiliation was an inevitable step toward His exaltation, and that exaltation was required to bring the creation into consummate submission, as well as granting salvation to the human family.

Reasons for Christ's Passion (Hebrews 2:10–11a)—*"For it was fitting that he, for whom and by whom all things exist, in bringing many sons to glory, should make the pioneer of their salvation perfect through suffering"* (Hebrews 2:10) ties into God's freely ordained plan of salvation. Hebrews stresses the connection between Savior and saved, Son and sons, Sanctifier and sanctified, between a Pioneer entering the heavenly world and those who are destined to follow Him there, between Christ glorified by God and children led by God into glory, and here between a suffering Christ and His human brothers and sisters. *"For he who sanctifies and those who are sanctified have all one origin"* (Hebrews 2:11). Does *common origin* mean descent from Adam, or Abraham, or from God? All three interpretations are possible; although the context here makes it probable that a community of nature rather than origin is intended. The interpretation then would be all have one nature that is a common humanity.

Notice there are two parallel sets of contrasts: "Christ–salvation–life" with "devil–sin–death." *"He himself likewise partook of the same nature, that through <u>death</u> he might destroy him who has <u>the power of death</u>, that is, the <u>devil</u>"* (Hebrews 2:14). By becoming man and suffering death, Jesus mysteriously undoes the consequence of sin and the power of Satan, gaining eternal life for us in the process (Romans 6:3–11). For those who are with Christ, spiritual death no longer causes the anguish, which is bondage. This paragraph comes to a conclusion in Hebrews 2:17–18 in the sense that Jesus had to be like His brethren, tempted and tried like them, and compassionate with them. *"He had to be made like his brethren in every respect, so that he might become a merciful and faithful high priest in the service of God, to make expiation for the sins of the people"* (Hebrews 2:17). This verse announces a central theme of the entire epistle, that of Christ our High Priest.

The required condition for becoming a high priest is quite surprising. In order for anyone to attain the dignity of a high priest the Old Testament prescribed ritual ceremonies of setting apart (Exodus 28; Leviticus 8–9), and it precluded any contact with a dead person (Leviticus 21:11). In contrast, the path that Christ was to follow was that of being in total resemblance of us mortals to the point of suffering and death. Implicitly, the sacred writer makes us understand that it was not only the Son's relationship with

His Father from all eternity that made Him a priest, but rather a close relationship with us in His incarnation that made mediation between God and man possible. Hence, only the glorified Lord possesses the necessary quality to be the eternal High Priest, and to bridge the gap between God and humanity that was caused by original sin and actual sin.

> He saw us bowed down to the ground, perishing, tyrannized by death; and He had mercy. To make reconciliation for the sins of the people, so that He might be a merciful and faithful High Priest. But what does "faithful" mean? True, able; for the only faithful High Priest is the Son, able to deliver from their sins those whose High Priest He is.
>
> (Saint John Chrysostom [344–407 AD]
> *Homilies on the Epistle to the Hebrews*, 5)

> This is the way, beloved, in which we found our salvation, Jesus Christ, the High Priest of our offerings, the defender and helper of our weakness. Through Him we fix our gaze on the heights of heaven; through Him we see the reflection of the faultless and lofty countenance of God; through Him the eyes of our heart were opened; through Him our foolish and darkened understanding shoots up to the light; through Him the Master willed that we should taste of deathless knowledge; who, being the brightness of His majesty, is as much greater than the angels as the more glorious name which He has inherited.
>
> (Saint Clement of Rome, [+99AD]
> *Letter to the Corinthians*, 36, 1)

1. What can you learn from these passages?

Hebrews 1:1–3
CCC 65
CCC 102
CCC 320
CCC 2777

2. How does Jesus rank compared to the angels?

Hebrews 1:5–13
Philippians 2:9–11
CCC 331, 333

3. Where can you find the glory and majesty of God?

Ephesians 1:20 or Colossians 1:15–20
Hebrews 1:1–3
1 Peter 3:21–22

* When and where have you best appreciated the majesty of God?

4. What can you learn about angels?

Hebrews 1:7
CCC 329

5. What can you learn about God's throne?

Psalm 45:6–7
Hebrews 1:8–9

6. When and how did God create the world?

Genesis 1:1
John 1:1–3
Hebrews 1:10
CCC 291

* What is your favorite part of God's creation?

7. What will endure and what will perish?

Psalm 102:26–28
Hebrews 1:11–12

8. What does Psalm 2:7 foretell?

9. By what name do we call Jesus Christ? Why? What does this title mean?

Hebrews 1:10
CCC 446
CCC 449

* List some titles of God that you use in your personal prayer.

10. What did the early believers hear?

Hebrews 2:1–3
2 Peter 1:16–18

* When did you first hear the proclamation of the Gospel in a clear way?

11. How does one come to salvation?

Hebrews 2:3–4
CCC 156

12. What does Psalm 8:4–6 foretell?

13. Explain Jesus' authority. Matthew 28:18

14. What is the order of Christ's authority? 1 Corinthians 15:25–28

15. Why did Jesus have to die?

Hebrews 2:9–14
CCC 609, 624, 629

16. How does Jesus see you and include you?

Hebrews 2:13
Hebrews 2:17
CCC 2602, 2779

17. What name does Jesus give to you in John 15:15?

*How can you come to feel a closer friendship with Jesus?

18. What does Jesus do and how does he do it?

Isaiah 25:8 or Hosea 13:14
2 Timothy 1:10
Hebrews 2:14–17
CCC 635

19. What hope can you find in 1 Corinthians 15:51–58?

20. Can you find help in trials or temptation? Hebrews 2:18, 1 Corinthians 10:13

*What is the most effective way that you have found to overcome temptation?

Chapter 9

God's Promise
Hebrews 3–5

For the word of God is living and active,
sharper than any two-edged sword,
piercing to the division of soul and spirit, of joints and marrow,
and discerning the thoughts and intentions of the heart.
Hebrews 4:12

Moses, a type of Christ's fidelity (Hebrews 3:1–6)—Our call is heavenly because it belongs to the order of heavenly reality and because of its goal, *"And this is eternal life, that they know you the only true God, and Jesus Christ whom you have sent"* (John 17:3). Christ becomes the pledge for our ascension into heaven. Jesus is an Apostle insofar as He is the principal One sent by God the Father. The priesthood of Christ and His mission in this world are part of our confession, the expression of our faith. *"[Moses] is entrusted with all my house"* (Numbers 12:7) forms the backdrop for the example of Jesus, *"He was faithful to him who appointed him, just as Moses also was faithful in God's house"* (Hebrews 3:2). Moses was faithful in the house of God, leading the Chosen People, as a servant and witness to *"the things that were to be spoken later"* (Hebrews 3:5) until the ultimate word came through the Son. Yet He who establishes the house is greater than he who serves in it, so Christ, the Son of God who built the house—in fulfillment of Nathan's prophecy (1 Chronicles 17:12–14)—surpasses Moses the servant, and His fidelity is greater. Recall that Miriam and Aaron contested the authority of Moses as God's accredited spokesman. We Christians are the people of God if we are faithful, that is, if we do not abandon our religion with the assurance and hope it gives. The two notions of fidelity and fulfillment will be developed in what follows.

Exhortation to personal fidelity (Hebrews 3:7–19)—Christians should imitate the faithfulness of the Lord. *"O that today you would listen to his voice! Harden not your hearts, as at Meribah, as on the day at Massah in the wilderness, when your fathers tested me, and put me to the proof, though they had seen my work"* (Psalm 95:7–8) serves as the basis for the warning to the new Chosen People against repeating the infidelity of the Israelites in the desert. Unbelieving does not so much refer to a lack of faith as a refusal of fidelity, an act of disobedience, an apostasy by which one falls away from the living God. *"Exhort one another every day, as long as it is called 'today,'"* (Hebrews 3:13) carries a Jewish overtone of a time of decision. Cassiodorus said that "today" means that we must listen to spiritual advice every day. *"For we share in Christ, if only we hold our first confidence firm to the end"* (Hebrews 3:14) encourages us to keep up the strong faith that was felt right after conversion. The original Greek *hypostasis* translated here as "confidence" or "assurance" really means the objective grounds for confidence. A number of rhetorical questions are presented to recall the Exodus and desert experience of Israel, the general sin of the people led by Moses and their eventual exclusion from the promised rest because of their disobedience and unbelief.

Heavenly rest (Hebrews 4:1–14)—The Good News (Greek *evangelizein*) cannot save the hearer if it is not met with faith. The rest promised was to have been in an earthly place, yet now the People of the New Covenant are given the promise of an eternal rest, which is in heaven, if only they remain faithful to the all-knowing God. *"Therefore, while the promise of entering his rest remains, let us fear lest any of you be judged to have failed to reach it"* (Hebrews 4:1) signals the freedom to make a decision. We are energized to enter that rest in the present and future, which is likened to the repose of God after the work of creation. This idea had given rise to the Jewish concept of a messianic sabbath. Saint Augustine said that only in God could the human heart rest. And Saint John Chrysostom said that lack of faith prevents us from resting in God. Although the Israelites in the wilderness failed to reach the promised rest, God has now established another "today" in which the members of His Church can accept or reject His promise. The repose that Joshua gave the Israelites by leading them into Canaan did not compare to the heavenly rest that God promises now.

The highly poetic conclusion has a strophe: *"For the word of God is living and active, sharper than any two-edged sword, piercing to the division of soul and spirit, of joints and marrow, and discerning the thoughts and intentions of the heart"* (Hebrews 4:12) and antistrophe: *"And before him no creature is hidden, but all are open and laid bare to the eyes of him with whom we have to do"* (Hebrews 4:13). The power of God's word (Hebrew *dabar*) filled with dynamic efficacy is employed to indicate God's immanence in the world of humanity in its capacity of discernment of spirits. Creation is faced with God's word and is ultimately accountable to Him. Jesus the High Priest, who has entered the heavenly sanctuary, provides the main motive for holding fast to our profession of faith.

Our compassionate High Priest (Hebrews 4:15–5:10)—Christ, the heavenly High Priest, in complete sympathy with our misery, is the source of our confidence. So let us turn to Him in every need. The divine throne that once frightened sinners *"I saw the Lord sitting upon a throne … And I said: 'Woe is me! For I am lost'"* (Isaiah 6:1, 5) has become the throne of grace that believers can approach with absolute trust: *"Let us then with confidence draw near to the throne of grace, that we may receive mercy"* (Hebrews 4:16). First, Saint Paul describes the function and calling of every priest, and then demonstrates the fulfillment of those conditions in Christ. Saint Paul looks to the Old Testament and its types to find mirrored therein images of Jesus. Actually, the Greek word for High Priest entered Jewish Greek quite late and was originally the title of an official during the Seleucid government in the second century BC. In the Greek Old Testament (the *Septuagint*) it occurs almost exclusively in 1 and 2 Maccabees. The letter to the Hebrews appears to have chosen High Priest because it is more becoming of Christ's dignity than the simple term priest, and because of the Old Testament connection He will establish.

A priest was to be chosen from among the people he represented (Exodus 28:1; Numbers 8:6), but Christ is able to represent all mankind. Needless to say, we have here an allusion to the Incarnation as the moment of His priestly calling and consecration, which eloquently took place in the splendid cathedral of the Virgin-Mother's womb, in the presence of His Father and of the Holy Spirit, as well as the archangel Gabriel! The Son of God was not always a priest, but became a priest when coming as the Son of Man. From then onwards it will be the God-Man to mediate worthily between His Father and His brethren by offering gifts and sacrifices and thereby atoning for sins. Obviously, there are other implied purposes of sacrificial worship like adoration, thanksgiving and petition.

> [When, because of their greater crimes, men] were in greater need of help, greater help was given them; and this was the Word Himself ... the unchangeable Image, the Rule and Word of the Father. To his own image He came, and took on flesh for the sake of flesh, and mingled Himself with an intelligent soul for the sake of my soul, purifying like by Like. In all except sin He was made Man. Conceived by the Virgin who was first purified in soul and body by the Spirit, for it was needful that birth be honored and that virginity be honored even more, He then came forth as God with that which He had assumed, one from two opposites, flesh and spirit, of which the one was deifying, the other deified.
>
> (Saint Gregory Nazianzen, [330–389 AD], *On The Theophany*, 38, 8)

"He can deal gently with the ignorant and wayward" (Hebrews 5:2) may be difficult to understand. To deal gently or to have compassion may not convey the idea of the original Greek (*metriopathein*) adequately. To the ancient Hellenistic mentality "feeling" (*pathos*) was considered unseemly for great men; but Hebrews finds the opposite "lack of feeling" (*apatheia*), which the Stoics held desirable, too severe for Christ, all the more so in a letter seeking to console people and exhort them to carry on in hardship. So the sacred author uses "have compassion in the middle" or "feel with measure," mysteriously alluding to our Lord's divine capacity of humanly and at the same time divinely redeeming us from all suffering and even death. In one word, Jesus has an unmatched ability to humbly relate to sinners. Surprisingly, however, His priestly eyes perceive them sympathetically in the best possible light. They are merely ignorant and wayward, beset with weakness, but not intrinsically evil or of hardened hearts. Besides, (a) human nature, and (b) compassion as priestly prerequisites there must also exist, (c) a divine calling, a priestly vocation, just as Aaron was called by God (Leviticus 8:1–2; Sirach 45:7). God and God alone can confer the priesthood especially of the New Covenant.

A concrete application to the person of Christ commences, beginning with the quality mentioned last. His divine calling is proven by two psalm citations, the first already adduced in *"You are my Son, today I have begotten you"* (Hebrews 1:5), and the second to be the *leit-motif* (main theme) of Hebrews 7. In the Apostolic Age *"You are my son, today I have begotten you"* (Psalm 2:7) was seen as pointing to the glorified Lord in His

Ascension and Seating at the Father's right hand, and this is precisely the Christological sense it is given in Hebrews in its additional emphasis on the link between this exaltation and Christ's priesthood. To bring both together he immediately complements and illuminates *"You are my son, today I have begotten you"* (Psalm 2:7), with *"You are a priest for ever according to the order of Melchizedek"* (Psalm 110:4). The declaratory formula "You are" contained in both verses shows that it is the glorified Jesus who is formally declared Priest by God. His priesthood flows not from His Passion alone but from His Passion crowned with His Exaltation, for both perfect His priestly life and sacrifice. Interestingly, the sacred writer omits the details defined by the old ritual (Levitical origin, ritual bath, vestments, anointing, animal sacrifices) to prepare the reader for the newness of Christ's priesthood according to the order of Melchizedek.

Many commentators have usually seen only the Passion of Christ in *"In the days of his flesh, Jesus offered up prayers and supplications, with loud cries and tears, to him who was able to save him from death, and he was heard for his godly fear. Although he was a Son, he learned obedience through what he suffered; and being made perfect he became the source of eternal salvation to all who obey him"* (Hebrews 5:7–9), but His glorification is here, too. Our Savior, faced with imminent suffering and death, prayed to His Father who was able to save Him from tasting death. *"Now is my soul troubled. And what shall I say? 'Father, save me from this hour? No, for this purpose I have come to this hour. Father, glorify your name … and I, when I am lifted up from the earth, will draw all men to myself'"* (John 12:27, 32). But, this deliverance went beyond all expectation in that His Father even delivered Him from the cold and permanent grip of death in His Resurrection.

Stunningly, although Jesus was already a loyal Son, He learned obedience—humanly speaking—in His acceptance of suffering. Because of this, combined with His filial reverence toward the Father's will, He was heard, then exalted in glory, thereby being made perfect, and becomes a fountain of salvation to all who obey Him. God now designates (literally, "publicly proclaims") Christ in His exalted humanity a High Priest. All of this results from His establishment in everlasting dominion with His Passion and Resurrection as prerequisites. In this light, the phrase *"Christ did not exalt Himself"* (Hebrews 5:5) finds its full significance. As a further detail, the word "perfected" refers in the Old Testament to the rite of priestly consecration. Whereas, *"For it was fitting that he, for whom and by whom all things exist, in bringing many sons to glory, should make the pioneer of their salvation perfect through suffering"* (Hebrews 2:10) ties in with suffering only, here it becomes equivalent to suffering transformed and made luminous in glory. Amazingly, this new and eternal Priest, having reached His vocational perfection in His sacrifice, is now truly capable of bringing to perfection all those who trust in Him.

This extraordinary text brings out the paschal glorification of Jesus with a new depth and full light in connecting it with priestly mediation. The Christological hymn: *"Christ Jesus, who, though he was in the form of God, did not count equality with God a thing to be grasped, but emptied himself, taking the form of a servant, being born in the likeness of men. And being found in human form he humbled himself and became obedient unto death, even death on a cross. Therefore God has highly exalted him and bestowed on him the name which is above every name, that at the name of Jesus every knee should bow, in heaven and on earth and under the earth, and every tongue confess that Jesus Christ is Lord, to the glory of God the Father"* (Philippians 2:6–11), for example, does not mention this aspect. Although several other New Testament passages come close to it, such as Luke 24:46ff; Acts 5:30ff; Romans 4:25; 8:34; 1 John 2:1ff.

Passages of theological catechesis regularly alternate with moments of exhortation and encouragement in Hebrews. Saint Paul, fully aware of the torpor (dullness) of his readers, *"since you have become dull of hearing"* (Hebrews 5:11), strives to stir them to a more enthusiastic hope. He rebukes them for remaining at a level of Christian infancy when they should by now have grown to an adult stage of knowledge, *"For though by this time you ought to be teachers, you need some one to teach you again the first principles of God's word"* (Hebrews 5:12). One will have to make a spiritual effort rather than just an intellectual one in order to assimilate the substantial doctrine ahead, a teaching that is not comparable to milk given to infants *"I fed you with milk, not solid food; for you were not ready for it; and even yet you are not ready"* (1 Corinthians 3:2). Saint Peter gives a similar admonition. *"So put away all malice and all guile and insincerity and envy and all slander. Like newborn infants, long for the pure spiritual milk, that by it you may grown up to salvation; for you have tasted the kindness of the Lord"* (1 Peter 2:1–3). Indeed, Christians are meant to aid others into their initiation into the mystery of Christ Jesus, and then to help them to grow into spiritual maturity.

You are called upon to help the younger generation to know Christ, to be able to follow Him and bear witness to Him. You are called to help the young take their place in the Church and society, and to overcome, in the light of the Gospel, the difficulties which they meet on their way to human and spiritual maturity.

Pope John Paul II, *Speech to Catechists*, October 4, 1998.

You have given proof of great evangelical courage in steering the People of God through numerous difficulties ... In all these situations, you tirelessly proposed the Church's teaching based on the Gospel, thus inspiring hope in your people's hearts ... I would like to warmly encourage each and every one of you to keep a balance in his apostolic life, making ample room for an intense spiritual life in order to create and reinforce his relations of friendship with Christ, so as to serve generously the section of the People of God entrusted to him and to proclaim the Kingdom of God to all ... In helping young people to acquire human and spiritual maturity, help them to discover God, help them discover that it is in the gift of themselves to the service of others that they will become freer and more mature!

Pope Benedict XVI, *Address of His Holiness*, September 20, 2007.

1. What comparisons can you make between Jesus and Moses? Hebrews 3:1–6

2. What confidence do you have that you are part of God's house?

Ephesians 3:8–12
Hebrews 3:6
CCC 2778

* How and when do you most feel confidence that you part of the family of God?

3. What can you learn from the following passages?

Exodus 17:2–7
Psalm 95:7–11
Hebrews 3:7–13

* Is there a time in your life when you were hard-hearted?

4. What advice can you find in Hebrews 3:12–15?

5. What precludes someone from entering into God's rest? Hebrews 3:18–19

6. Describe some aspects of the sabbath rest from these passages:

Genesis 2:2
Hebrews 4:1–9
CCC 2172

*In what ways do you provide a sabbath rest for yourself each Sunday?

7. Explain the significance and spiritual senses of God's Word.

Wisdom 18:15–16
Ephesians 6:17
Hebrews 4:12
CCC 117

8. Describe some aspects of divine providence.

Hebrews 4:13
CCC 302

* Give an example of divine providence in your own life.

9. Explain some characteristics of Jesus from these sources:

Hebrews 4:14–15
CCC 612

10. Discuss the encouragement found in Hebrews 4:16.

11. Who is Melchizedek? Genesis 14:18–20

12. Who has a right to become a priest? Hebrews 5:4–5; CCC 1578

13. How does Jesus achieve our salvation?

Hebrews 5:7–9
CCC 617
CCC 2606

14. What truth does Jesus demonstrate? 1 Samuel 15:22

15. What did Jesus do prior to His Passion?

Mark 14:35–39
Hebrews 5:7

16. By whom and how is death transformed? CCC 1009

* What hope does this provide in contemplating the death of a loved one, or even your own personal death?

** How and in light of what truth could you comfort someone who is grieving the death of a loved one?

17. Explain the one priesthood of Christ?

Hebrews 5:5–10
CCC 1544

18. Identify the problem faced in Hebrews 5:11–12.

19. Compare the following verses:

Hebrews 5:12–14
1 Corinthians 3:1–3

20. Identify an ultimate goal in the following:

Colossians 1:28; 4:12
Hebrews 5:14

* List some ways in which you could grow in Christian maturity?

Chapter 10
Jesus the High Priest
Hebrews 6–7

For it was fitting that we should have such a high priest,
holy, blameless, unstained, separated from sinners, exalted above the heavens.
He has no need, like those high priests, to offer sacrifices daily,
first for their own sins and then for those of the people;
he did this once for all when he offered up himself.
Hebrews 7:26–27

The peril of falling away (Hebrews 6:1–20)—Here is an exhortation to abandon the elementary phase of faith for an adult form of believing, and to be attentive to the difficult teaching ahead. Dead works lead to spiritual death. What is enigmatic is the plural "baptisms" in Hebrews 6:2, for Christians knew of a single baptism. Perhaps it points toward the distinction between Christian baptism and that of John the Baptist or even certain Jewish ritual ablutions. Also, the laying on of hands in the Bible indicates the conferment of a ministry and the giving of the Holy Spirit (Acts 8:17–19; 19:6; 1 Timothy 4:14; 5:22; 2 Timothy 1:6). The topics listed in these verses must have played an important part in the catechesis of neophytes, that is, those who were preparing to be baptized or had recently joined the Church.

> Now may God and the Father of our Lord Jesus Christ, and the Eternal High Priest Himself, Jesus Christ, the Son of God, build you up in faith and in truth, in meekness perfect and without resentment, in patience and in long-suffering, in endurance, and in purity. May He set your lot and portion among His saints, — and ourselves along with you, and all others under heaven who in the future will believe in our Lord Jesus Christ, and in His Father, who raised Him from the dead.
>
> Saint Polycarp of Smyrna, (60- 155 AD), *Second Letter to the Philippians*, 12, 2.

Saint Paul now confronts his readers with another, even more consequential, choice: apostasy and ultimate failure, or perseverance and hope. Once a person has become a Christian and then fallen away, he or she cannot be restored again to repentance. The text does not deny the chance of repentance for sin in general, but addresses the case of someone who has deliberately turned away from Christ in disobedience and hardness of heart, disdaining the redemption wrought by the Lord. This offense compares to the sin against the Holy Spirit in the synoptic Gospels (Matthew 12:31ff; Mark 3:22–30; Luke 12:10), in which one's free will opposes the grace of God. Hebrews speaks to Christians faced with active persecution, forced to worship emperors and pagan gods accompanied by a curse against Christ Himself and thereby renounce their faith. Thus, in order to prevent widespread apostasy during those trying times, the letter uses strong pastoral language to encourage faithfulness, and as such it is inspired and inerrant.

The expression "enlightened" may relate to the Sacrament of Baptism, also known for many centuries as "illumination" (*photismos*), as well as a heavenly gift, a possible hint at the Eucharistic species of bread and wine. *"For it is impossible to restore again to repentance those who have once been enlightened, who have tasted the heavenly gift, and have become partakers of the Holy Spirit, and have tasted the goodness of the word of God and the powers of the age to come, if they then commit apostasy, since they crucify the Son of God on their own account and hold him up to contempt* (Hebrews 6:4–6). A rhetorical contrast is well made: the evocation of the Christian joy and enthusiasm followed by the dark failure of the apostate, similar to fruitful and barren land respectively. God's unfailing promise gives the firmest grounds for our hope. The two unchanging things are God's promise and the oath by which He has sworn. What is behind the curtain is the inner sanctuary, which is heaven, based on the image of the veil that separated the Holy from the innermost Holy of Holies in the temple of Jerusalem. Every Christian is moored to it as it were with the anchor of faith. Now that the sacred writer has concluded his admonition bringing his readers to an earnest frame of mind, he is ready to take up his more arduous doctrine.

> When we are baptized, we are enlightened. Being enlightened, we are adopted as sons. Adopted as sons, we are made perfect. Made perfect, we are become immortal … This work is variously called grace, illumination, perfection, and washing. It is a washing by which we are cleansed of sins; a gift of grace by which the punishments due our sins are remitted; an illumination by which we behold that holy light of salvation—that is, by which we see God clearly; and we call that perfection which leaves nothing lacking. Indeed, if a man know God, what more does he need? … Because God is perfect, the gifts He bestows are perfect.
>
> Saint Clement of Alexandria, (150–216 AD),
> *The Instructor of Children*, 1, 6, 26.

The priestly order of Melchizedek (Hebrews 7:1–10)—The goal of this chapter is to focus on the transcendence of Christ's sublime priesthood, using the methods of rabbinic exegesis (traditional Jewish interpretation of the Torah) as well as Christian typology, seeing the Old Testament fulfilled in the New and in Christ. The priesthood of Melchizedek is superior to that of Aaron and the Levites in a twofold argument: (a) he who receives a tithe is greater than he who pays it, and (b) he who blesses is greater than he who is blessed. Now, in their ancestor, Abraham, the Levites paid tithes to Melchizedek and were blessed by him. Therefore, the latter excels the former and, by implication, his priesthood is greater than theirs. The entire thought is founded on the episode narrated in Genesis 14:17–20.

Hebrews offers an original clarification of names that is not given in Genesis 14, namely that Melchizedek is the "King of Righteousness" and the "King of Peace" (*Salem*), a royal title with a messianic resonance. Since Genesis reveals nothing about Melchizedek's origin or death, Hebrews uses this as an argument with Christ in mind to conclude that he had an ancestry, which was mysteriously supernatural, and an immortal life, resembling the Son of God. Hence, Melchizedek is a *type*, or foreshadowing, of Christ and His eternal priesthood.

Another High Priest (Hebrews 7:11–28)—Jesus Christ as High Priest is shown to be the *antetype* of Melchizedek, the Old Testament *type*. The priesthood of Jesus is not a mere continuation of that of Aaron and the Levites as it was transmitted by way of family lineage. It is of another order: (a) Christ is of the non-priestly tribe of Judah, and (b) but is after the order of Melchizedek. This change was necessary due to the imperfection and inefficacy of the Old Testament spirituality. Priesthood and Law had to undergo a profound transformation to reach true holiness, not depending any longer on heredity but on eternal life. God swore an oath to give eternal value to the new institution. *"On the one hand, a former commandment is set aside because of its weakness and uselessness (for the law made nothing perfect); on the other hand, a better hope is introduced, through which we draw near to God … This makes Jesus the surety of a better covenant"* (Hebrews 7:18–19, 22). It is remarkable that not only the former priesthood is contested but that the entire Law is challenged, vigorously reopening the Pauline polemic against the Old Law. Not the juridical vocabulary of "justification" is used here, but instead the priestly vocabulary of perfection. Thus, the Law cannot make perfect (Hebrews 7:19; 10:1), just as it cannot justify (Galatians 3:11; Romans 3:20).

If multiplicity and change are traits of imperfection, then oneness and immutability are signs of perfection: the old priests were numerous and they died, while Christ is One and His priestly ministry remains forever. His salvation is not transitory but permanent, proving its divine efficaciousness. *"Consequently he is able for all time to save those who draw near to God through him, since he always lives to make intercession for them"* (Hebrews 7:25). This intercession illustrates Jesus' appearance in the presence of His heavenly Father after His Ascension, and the expiation brought about by His glorified wounds. He is the eternal Mediator between all of humanity and His Father's heart.

"For it was fitting that we should have such a high priest, holy, blameless, unstained, separated from sinners, exalted above the heavens. He has no need, like those high priests, to offer sacrifices daily, first for his own sins and then for those of the people; he did this once for all when he offered up himself. Indeed, the law appoints men in their weakness as high priests, but the word of the oath, which came later than the law, appoints a Son who has been made perfect for ever" (Hebrews 7:26–28). This conclusion expresses Saint Paul's contemplative admiration before the icon of the ideal High Priest, Jesus, in His insuperable sanctity, heavenliness and permanence, infinitely outshining the sinful nature of the earthly priests and their sacrifices from of old. Jesus is the High Priest *par excellence*, the Holy of Holies, the Most High God, who came to redeem the world.

> Just as in the form of God, He lacked nothing of the divine nature and its fullness, so too in the form of man there was nothing lacking in Him, by the absence of which He might have been judged as imperfect man; for He came to save the whole man. It would not have been fitting for One who accomplished a perfect work in others to allow anything imperfect in Himself. If something was lacking in His humanity, He did not redeem the whole man; and if He did not redeem the whole man, He was a deceiver when He declared that He had come to save the whole man. But, He did not deceive, because "It is not possible for God to lie." Because He came therefore to save and redeem the whole man, it follows that He took upon Himself the whole man, and that His humanity was perfect.
>
> Saint Ambrose of Milan, (333–397 AD), *Letter to Sabinus*, 48, 32, 5.

The late Pope John Paul II gave a catechesis on Jesus Christ, Messiah Priest in a general audience in February 1987, which shows the relationship between Jesus and the priest Melchizedek. Although Jesus was not of the priestly tribe of Levi, but of the tribe of Judah, Jesus truly fulfills the mission of priestly-king-Messiah.

> The paschal events revealed the true meaning of the "Messiah-King" and of the "king-priest after the order of Melchizedek," which [while] present in the Old Testament found its fulfillment in the mission of Jesus of Nazareth. ... The Letter to the Hebrews states clearly and convincingly that Jesus Christ has fulfilled with his whole life, and especially with the sacrifice of the cross, all that was written in the messianic tradition of divine revelation. His priesthood is situated in reference to the ritual service of the priests of the old covenant, which he surpasses as priest and victim. God's eternal design, which provides for the institution of the priesthood in the history of the covenant, is fulfilled in Christ.
>
> According to the Letter to the Hebrews, the messianic task is symbolized by the figure of Melchizedek. There we read that by God's will *"another priest arises in the likeness of Melchizedek, not according to a legal requirement concerning bodily descent but by the power of an indestructible life"* (Hebrews 7:15). It is therefore an eternal priesthood.
>
> The Church, faithful guardian and interpreter of these and other texts contained in the New Testament, has reaffirmed over and over again the truth of the Messiah-priest, as witnessed, for example, by the Ecumenical Council of Ephesus (431 AD), that of Trent (1562 AD), and in our own time, the Second Vatican Council (1962–1965).
>
> An evident witness of this truth is found in the Eucharistic sacrifice which by Christ's institution the Church offers every day under the species of bread and wine, "after the order of Melchizedek."
>
> Pope John Paul II, *General Audience*, February 18, 1987

1. What is the significance of the laying on of hands?

Hebrews 6:1–2
Acts 8:17
CCC 699
CCC 1288

* On what occasions did a bishop, priest, or lay person lay hands on you?

2. What happens when we deny Our Lord?

Hebrews 6:6
CCC 598

3. Explain the seriousness and consequences of denouncing Christ.

Mark 3:28–29
Hebrews 6:4–6
2 Peter 2:20–21
CCC 679

* Explain the difference between falling back into sin and apostasy. Give examples.

4. Explain God's promise to Abraham.

Genesis 22:16–17	
Hebrews 6:13–15	

5. Describe the Christian virtue found in these passages.

Hebrews 6:19–20	
1 Peter 1:21	
CCC 1820	

* What practical means can you employ to grow in the virtue of hope?

6. Identify the common practice described in these passages:

Genesis 14:20	
Malachi 3:10	
Hebrews 7:2–5	

7. How many references to tithing can you find in Hebrews 7:1–9?

8. What happens when God's people are not generous? Malachi 3:8–9

9. What results from people's generosity to God? Malachi 3:10–12

* How generous are you to God? Have you ever tithed your time or money?

10. What was the priestly tribe of the Jews? Hebrews 7:11

11. From which tribe of Israel did Jesus come? Matthew 1:1–3; Hebrews 7:14

12. Explain the power of Jesus' life.

Hebrews 7:16
CCC 648

13. Identify a characteristic of God in these passages:

Malachi 3:6
Hebrews 7:21

14. For how long will Jesus be a priest and intercessor?

Hebrews 7:24
CCC 519

15. Explain Christ's sacrifice in light of the Eucharist.

Hebrews 7:25–27
CCC 1364
CCC 1366

* In what practical ways could you be more attentive at Mass?

** How could you demonstrate Jesus' kingship or Lordship in your life?

16. What is Jesus able to do for you?

Hebrews 7:25
CCC 662
CCC 2634
CCC 2741

17. Describe some things Jesus does for you.

John 10:10–11
Romans 8:33–34
1 John 2:1–2
Revelation 1:17–18

18. List five characteristics of Jesus from Hebrews 7:26.

19. What does Christ do in the liturgy?

Hebrews 7:27
CCC 1085

20. What trait of God the Father does Jesus display? Matthew 5:48; Hebrews 7:28

Monthly Social Activity

This month, your small group will meet for coffee, tea, or a simple breakfast, lunch, or dessert in someone's home. Pray for this social event and for the host or hostess. Try, if at all possible, to attend.

After a short prayer and some time for small talk, write a few sentences about some mature Christians who you know and admire. Make sure that everyone has time to share.

Examples

◆ *My mother was an exemplary example of Christian kindness and prayerfulness for me. She always had room for one more in our house and around our table.*

◆ *There was a teacher in my school who always looked out for the needy and had an encouraging word for each of us.*

◆ *My boss showed me how you could be a faithful Catholic in the business world without compromising your principles.*

Chapter 11
Worship
Hebrews 8–10

Therefore, brethren, since we have confidence to enter the sanctuary by the blood of Jesus, by the new and living way which he opened for us through the curtain, that is, through his flesh, and since we have a great priest over the house of God, let us draw near with a true heart in full assurance of faith, with our hearts sprinkled clean from an evil conscience and our bodies washed with pure water.
Hebrews 10:19–22

Mediator of a new Covenant (Hebrews 8:1–13)—After a brief introduction, the inefficacy of the old priesthood is explained, followed by an eloquent explanation of the perfect priesthood of Christ. The old priestly institution and liturgy were earthly. Christ would not be an earthly priest because there was no lack of those who had "something to offer." A sanctuary where sacrifice is efficacious had to belong to the heavenly realm, yet the priests of the Old Law served only "a copy and shadow" of this sanctuary, not the genuine, spiritual one. Although the ancient cultic order was not completely without meaning, it had value only in view of the future plenitude of the celestial realities. Hebrews then recalls Exodus 25, when God revealed to Moses the pattern (also called *archetype*) of the tabernacle on Sinai. This wilderness sanctuary, by the way, had caused Jewish apocalyptic literature to develop the concept of a heavenly temple in which angels minister (see also Revelation 11:19; 15:5ff; 16:1).

Covenant and priesthood are inextricably interwoven; when one is changed the other must change as well. The nature of this new Covenant including the better promises pervading it is explained through the unique prophecy of Jeremiah: *"Behold, the days are coming, says the LORD, when I will make a new covenant with the house of Israel and the house of Judah, not like the covenant which I made with their fathers when I took them by the hand to bring them out of the land of Egypt, my covenant which they broke, and I showed myself their Master, says the LORD. But this is the covenant which I will make with the house of Israel after those days, says the LORD: I will put my law within them, and I will write it upon their hearts; and I will be their God, and they shall be my people"* (Jeremiah 31:31–33). The law of a new Covenant will be inscribed in the very heart and mind of the individual person. Its terms will be implemented by willing consent and personal responsibility, not fearfully or reluctantly. By the very act of uttering the word "new" God has effectively made the first dispensation obsolete.

The earthly and heavenly sanctuaries (Hebrews 9:1–28)—Hebrews provides types (or images) for the heavenly liturgy, and provides a contrast between the older order of salvation and the new transcendent one. Hebrews 9:1–5 draws heavily on Exodus 25–26

(Exodus 16:33; Num 17:2–5) in picturing the desert tabernacle. The most relevant item is the separation into two tents: an outer one, the Holy Place (*Sanctum*), and an inner one, the Holy of Holies (*Sancta Sanctorum*). Allusion then is made of the Day of Atonement (*Yom Kippur*, Leviticus 16), only to maintain its preliminary and imperfect nature. Ordinary priests came into the outer tent on a daily basis to offer incense, but only the Day of Atonement, once a year, did the high priest—and he alone—enter the Holy of Holies to confect the sacrifice of reparation first for his own sins and then for those of the people. For the sacred author the very continuity of this activity underscored its imperfection, and this is the main reason for their mention here. Additionally, the singular liturgy of that day with the sprinkling of blood furnished a helpful image for the work of redemption in Christ Jesus.

"By this the Holy Spirit indicates that the way into the sanctuary is not yet opened as long as the outer tent is still standing" (Hebrews 9:8). The Holy Spirit is the interpreter of Old Testament realities! Access to the sanctuary was closed yet for the people at large, and is only opened as a result of Christ's sacrificial liturgy. Tellingly, the Greek original reads "manifested": the way into the New Sanctuary, therefore, needed not only to be opened, but also to be manifested by the Son in the completion of revelation. Moreover, unlike the earthly copy, the first tabernacle, the heavenly place is not divided into two parts. The arrangements of old stopped at the flesh, remaining in a material order outside the dominion of the spirit, without effect on the innermost person. On the contrary, the New Covenant, the time of reformation, will penetrate the depth of the inner being, cleansing our consciences.

The perfection of Christ's priesthood is contrasted with the shortcomings of the old order. The great barrier to our access to God is sin, and the letter utilizes details of the *Yom Kippur* ritual to draw parallels with the heavenly liturgy, that is, Jesus' work of salvation. It is no longer the high priest who sprinkles the blood of animals unto the propitiatory, or mercy seat, to reconcile the people to God. The crucified Christ Himself became the Victim on earth—priest, victim and altar at the same time—and in His Ascension entered the heavenly Sanctuary, not made with hands, to bring about total reconciliation in perpetuity in His own blood. Christ passed the upper cosmic heavens to present Himself as Priest to His Father. Other passages also speak of the mysteriously divine and glorious body of the God-Man (John 1:14; 2:19–21; Mark 14:58; Colossians 2:9). His blood has acquired the necessary efficacy by being united to the Godhead. Hence, all of God's children now have access to the Father through the wounded (Passion + Death) and glorified (Resurrection + Ascension + Session) humanity of His Son (the Lamb, slain and standing, Revelation 5:6), once and for all! The Flesh and Blood of the Holy Eucharist emerges in these verses, and you also glimpse the Blessed Trinity: *"how much more shall the blood of Christ, who through the eternal Spirit offered himself without blemish to God, purify your conscience from dead works to serve the living God"* (Hebrews 9:14)!

"He entered once for all into the Holy Place, taking not the blood of goats and calves but his own blood, thus securing an eternal redemption" (Hebrews 9:12). This verse

emphasizes Christ's *transitus* (passage) as Mediator of the New Covenant. A last will and testament has no validity until the testator (the one issuing the will) has died; but Jesus, whose legacy is the New Testament, has by His death made the Covenant. This argument rests on the double meaning of the Greek *diatheke* meaning both "testament" and "covenant," showing that Christ's inheritance truly is an eternal Covenant and is actually given to us as a result of His death. The principle enunciated in Leviticus 17:11 using blood in making expiation for sins is broadened to a general axiom, that without bloodshed there is no forgiveness of sins. Saint Paul uses this Old Testament text to show the fittingness of the new dispositions, partial elements of the great mystery of Christ. The transitional Hebrews 9:23 highlights the dedication or inauguration of the heavenly sanctuary (see also 2 Maccabees 2:16–18; 10:3–5). Formerly the sanctuary was the focal point of the relations between God and Israel; if the people sinned, God abandoned the sanctuary or temple (Ezekiel 10:18ff; 11:22), but if the sanctuary was purified with the determined rite, the sins of the people were expiated (Leviticus 16:16–34) and the Lord returned to the sanctuary (Ezekiel 43:2–5; 44:4). This is the scriptural background of this and the following verses.

> Christ was offered once. By whom, was He offered? Quite evidently, by Himself. Here [Paul] shows that Christ was not Priest only, but also Victim and Sacrifice. Therein do we find the reason for the words *was offered*. *"He was offered once,"* [Paul] says, *"to take away the sins of many"* (Hebrews 9:28). Why does he say *of many* and not *of all*? Because not all have believed. He did indeed die for all, for the salvation of all, which was His part ... But He did not take away the sins of all men, because they did not will it.
>
> (Saint John Chrysostom, [344–407 AD],
> *Homilies on the Epistle to the Hebrews*, 17, 2)

The suffering and death of Christ mirrors the slaughter of the animal on the Day of Atonement. His *transitus* to the celestial world corresponds to the passage of the high priest into the temple's inner *Sanctum*, and now there remains the typology (meaning of Old Testament images) of the blood-sprinkling once the high priest had arrived in the Holy of Holies (Leviticus 16:14–16). By analogy, the consummation of Christ's saving work took place in the heavenly Holy of Holies at the moment of His glorification at His Father's right hand. Hebrews uses two further images to describe the Lord's work there: a) the appearance in the presence of God and b) the intercession. Wisdom literature had come to see expiatory activity in the Old Testament as intercession. Thus, the new High Priest is continuously interceding for us here on earth with His Father until He comes in glory. And once He appears a second time (*Parousia*)—just as Aaron emerged from the sanctuary after the sacrifice to bless the people—and takes us to Himself in heaven it will still be through Him that we are introduced to His Father.

The fruits of Christ's sacrifice (Hebrews 10:1–18)—The salvation in Christ possesses the "exact image" (literally "icon") of the celestial realities. Psalm 40:6–9 is cited to underline both the inability of ancient sacrifice to placate God, and the obedient will of His Son who pleased God. *"Sacrifices and offerings you have not desired, but a body have you prepared for me"* (Hebrews 10:5) is of great Christological relevance since it marks the first priestly act of the Son at the very instant of His conception in His Mother's womb, when He came into the world, expressing His willingness to use His body to offer Himself for all of us. This verse is a powerful reminder of the sanctity of human life from its natural beginning to its natural end! The interval between the two comings of Christ is characterized by the progressive subjection of the universe to His dominion, including His enemies who will be made His footstool. In the process the Sanctifier perfects all those who are sanctified. Since the sacrifice has been made once and for all, there remains only to apply it to the individual persons through the seven sacraments of the Church.

A call to persevere (Hebrews 10:19–39)—Jesus' body is both the way and the curtain that leads into the heavenly temple. Baptism is the sacrament that is behind the true heart, the assurance of faith, the sprinkling and cleansing of consciences. Baptism provides bodies and souls washed with pure water. We are also instructed regarding a strong sense for community life to encourage one another in love and good works *"all the more as you see the Day [of the Lord] draw near"* (Hebrews 10:25). The early Church hoped and expected an early return of Christ. Notice also the encouragement in practicing the theological virtues of faith, hope and love.

> Since man is of a twofold nature, composed of body and soul, the purification is twofold: the corporeal for the corporeal and the incorporeal for the incorporeal. The water cleanses the body, and the Spirit seals the soul. Thus, having our heart sprinkled by the Spirit and our body washed with pure water, we may draw near to God. When you go down into the water, then, regard not simply the water, but look for salvation through the power of the Holy Spirit. For without both you cannot attain to perfection. It is not I who say this, but the Lord Jesus Christ, who has the power in this matter.
>
> (Saint Cyril of Jerusalem, [315–386 AD], *Catechetical Lectures*, 3, 4)

Concerning apostasy, something warned about earlier, several additional details are now presented. Serious sin is done deliberately and with full knowledge of the truth. Those who do turn away become *"adversaries"* (Hebrews 10:27) who have *"spurned the Son of God"* and *"outraged the Spirit of grace"* (Hebrews 10:29), and thus render themselves hopeless. To deliberately turn away from God and reject His mercy, or to presume upon His mercy by continuing in apostasy is a fearful thing. Finally, the reader is given an insight into early Church persecution and Christian confidence and endurance.

1. What can you explain about priesthood and liturgy?

Hebrews 8:2–6
CCC 1069
CCC 1070

2. Explain the work of the New Law or New Covenant.

Romans 10:4
Galatians 3:24–27
Hebrews 8:8–10
CCC 1965
CCC 1966

3. Compare the following verses:

Jeremiah 31:33–34
Hebrews 8:8–10

4. How can you know the Lord? Hebrews 8:11–12

5. Name three things found in the Ark of the Covenant. Hebrews 9:4

6. What can you learn about the mercy seat?

Exodus 25:17–34
Hebrews 9:5
CCC 433

7. How does Christ relate to the temple and the treasury of the Church?

Hebrews 9:11–12
CCC 586
CCC 1476

8. Explain genuine efficacious sacrifice.

Hebrews 9:13–14
CCC 614
CCC 2100

9. What does Jesus do for your conscience? Hebrews 9:14

10. Explain the significance of Christ's coming and the New Covenant.

Hebrews 9:15
CCC 522
CCC 580
CCC 592

11. Where and for whom did Christ enter the sanctuary? Hebrews 9:24; CCC 519

12. Discuss some aspects of death from these passages:

Hebrews 9:27–28
CCC 1021
CCC 1017

* Are you afraid of death? What does the resurrection of the body mean for you?

13. Can the Law or priesthood bring about salvation? Hebrews 10:1–4; CCC 1540

14. How is God's will perfectly fulfilled?

Hebrews 10:7
CCC 2824

15. What then should we do? Hebrews 10:19–24

16. What things are encouraged in Hebrews 10:23–25?

17. Why do you go to Mass on Sundays?

Hebrews 10:25
CCC 2177
CCC 2178

18. Will everyone go to heaven? Hebrews 10:26–31

19. What do you need to obey God's will and receive the promise? Hebrews 10:36

20. What virtue must you have to persevere? Hebrews 10:38–39

Chapter 12

Faith and Endurance
Hebrews 11–13

Therefore, since we are surrounded by so great a cloud of witnesses,
let us also lay aside every weight, and sin which clings so closely,
and let us run with perseverance the race that is set before us,
looking to Jesus the pioneer and perfecter of our faith,
who for the joy that was set before him endured the cross, despising the shame,
and is seated at the right hand of the throne of God.
Hebrews 12:1–2

Faith (Hebrews 11:1–40)—When the letter to the Hebrews reflects on faith it does so with a markedly eschatological outlook. The faith of the Old Testament patriarchs and heroes is recalled. The beginning and end of this chapter put this ancestral faith in the eschatological framework, that is, looking forward to something not yet attained, even after the Advent of Christ. The way the traditions are presented is historical and transcendent at the same time, always having Christ as their key. *"Now faith is the assurance of things hoped for, the conviction of things not seen"* (Hebrews 11:1). This magnificent definition combines what faith actually is and how it is blended with hope. The substance (Greek *hypostasis*) of realities hoped for, as well as the proof (*elenchos*) of things not seen. Faith before Abraham is contemplated in the lives of Abel, Enoch, and Noah, always directed toward the future as well as things unseen. Only in faith do we grasp the meaning of everything visible and invisible as created by God in the beginning of time. An old Jewish tradition calls Abel the father of the just. Because Enoch pleased God he was transported to Him. Noah's obedient construction of the ark was an example of faith and a condemnation of the world.

> *Without faith it is impossible to please God* (Hebrews 11:16). For faith is the basis of all goods. Faith is the beginning of human salvation. Without faith no one can pertain to the number of the sons of God, because without [faith] neither will anyone obtain the grace of justification in this life nor attain eternal life in the future; and if anyone does not walk now in faith, he will not arrive at the actuality. Without faith every human labor is empty.
> (Saint Fulgence of Ruspe, (467–527 AD), *The Rule of Faith*, 1)

As Abraham was the supreme pattern of faith among the Jews, Paul now dwells at length on his faith. The great patriarch's faith is portrayed in his (a) obedience to the call of God to go in search of the Promised Land, (b) confidence in God's promise of offspring, and (c) willingness to sacrifice Isaac. Jewish traditions hold that Abraham first had faith, and that God rewarded him with visions of this world and the world to come. Abraham becomes a role model for our pilgrimage towards an unseen goal. The allusion to living in tents signifies the impermanence and instability of this present life, looking forward to that city which has foundations. Furthermore, faith is seen as the cause of Sarah's conception of Isaac. These ancient heroes died without receiving the promises but awaiting better ones, like Moses who dies outside the borders of the Promised Land. The sacred writer then resumes the example of individuals from Abraham to Joseph, with a certain theme of imminent death and concern for the future posterity, coupled with the hope in God's promise. According to a Jewish tradition Isaac was actually killed and brought back to life, which seems to harmonize with Hebrew's viewpoint. Thus, Isaac could then become a symbol both of Christ's death *and* Resurrection.

Faith from Moses to Joshua emerges. Examples of detachment from the pagan world, attachment to the community of believers, and constancy in temptation "suffered for the Christ" are lauded in Moses' life, and a reward is laid up for him. But then in Hebrews 11:32 the detailed series of examples is broken off in favor of a more general picture of the heroism of Israelites from the time of the Judges onward. Although *"they were sawn in two"* (Hebrews 11:37) is a torture not mentioned in the Old Testament, it is found in legends of the death of Isaiah. And now these last days have arrived, with Christ and all hopes are fulfilled. The idea of solidarity in redemption returns here. Patriarchs and Christians together take their place among *"the spirits of the just men made perfect"* (Hebrews 12:23).

> Faith, which the Greeks disparage and regard as useless and barbarous, is a voluntary preconception, the assent of piety; "the substance of things hoped for, the evidence of those things which are not seen," according to the divine Apostle. "For by it most especially did the men of old have testimony borne to them; and without faith it is impossible to please God." Others, however have defined faith as an intellectual assent to a thing unseen, since certainly the proof of a thing unknown is manifest assent … He, then, that believes in the Divine Scriptures with firm judgment, receives, in the voice of God, who gave the Scriptures, an unquestionable proof. Nor by proof does faith become more firm. Blessed, therefore, are those who have not seen and yet have believed.
>
> (Saint Clement of Alexandria, [150–216 AD], *Stromateis*, 2, 2, 8, 4)

The heroes of the past gained a reputation for faith, and to a certain extent, they realized the divine promises. But they did not live to see the promised Messiah. Without any fault of theirs, the supreme reward of faith was denied to them. It was reserved for a later date. But, now, along with us, they have entered into the full inheritance of faith. They are admitted into heaven through the messianic blessings brought about by Christ. Their faith has been perfected through Jesus.

Endurance (Hebrews 12:1–29)—The sacred author now turns to the present to encourage his audience to persevere in their own faith no matter what hardship it costs, like in a school of endurance. *"We are surrounded by so great a cloud of witnesses"* (Hebrews 12:1), spurring us on to victory. The One who provides an example is Jesus Himself, the pioneer and perfecter of our faith, who endured the cross, for the joy set before Him. Like any athlete putting himself in shape for a contest, the Christian must ready himself by arduous training, the program of which is drawn up by God. Christian life is to be inspired not only by Old Testament men and women of faith, but above all by Jesus, the Architect of Christian faith. Reflection on His suffering should give everyone courage to endure hardship and to continue the struggle. The exhortation to accept the discipline of the Lord comes from the Holy Scripture itself *"My son do not despise the LORD's discipline or be weary of his reproof"* (Proverbs 3:11), because God paternally educates and corrects us like a father who loves his children.

The believer is advised and admonished to strive for spiritual strength and avoid sin. We should attempt to live peaceably with our fellow men on earth and share in God's holiness. The use of Esau as an example of immorality and godlessness may sound surprising. However, late Jewish literature had built up a consistent tradition of Esau's loose morals. At last in detail the heavenly city appears, the goal of the Christian pilgrimage. At the same time the antithesis of the two Covenants is made with the symbolism of two mountains: Mount Sinai, where the Old Covenant was made, and Mount Zion, the mountain of the New Jerusalem. While Sinai is portrayed as a place of fear and dread, Zion is apocalyptic and eschatological, the focus of awesome spiritual realities and of communion with God, in an age, which is now, and at the same time is yet to be. This remarkably beautiful passage contrasts two great assemblies of people: the Israelites at Mount Sinai, and the Christians at Mount Zion. This will be further illustrated in the celestial liturgies in Revelation. There we find the firstborn enrolled in heaven, which are the elect in general. The literary climax of this paragraph is the presence of the divine Mediator and Eternal High Priest in consummation.

"See that you do not refuse him who is speaking" (Hebrews 12:25) refers to the Lord Himself. The reader is reminded of the great cosmic upheaval at the end of world history that will witness His coming as the definitive Judge of all people. The earth was shaken at Sinai, both heaven and earth will be shaken at the end of time, yet the transformation of passing things is already accomplished in the new kingdom established by Christ, which is the Church. But our share in it should not be taken lightly, for we can still lose it by turning away from God. Our worship should be made in reverence and awe, for if we fall away we may come to know and experience that God is a consuming fire.

Sacrifices that are pleasing to God (Hebrews 13:1–19)—Hebrews proceeds to suggest concrete practices of charity. *"Let brotherly love continue. Do not neglect to show hospitality to strangers, for thereby some have entertained angels unawares"* (Hebrews 13:1–2) recalls Old Testament examples of charity and hospitality (Genesis 18–19; Judges 13; Tobit 5:9; 7:1). Believers must also show attentiveness toward prisoners and those who are ill-treated. Marriage is to be kept undefiled, which is a most urgent message for our own days. Freedom from greed and contentedness are already part of the Wisdom tradition in the sense that they open us up to trust in God's loving providence (Matthew 6:34; Philippians 4:6; 1 Timothy 3:3; 6:6; 1 Peter 5:7).

Christians are now reminded to be faithful to orthodox teaching and worship. The leaders seem to point to the clergy who preached the authentic Gospel and provided examples of perseverance in faith until the end. *"Jesus Christ is the same yesterday and today and for ever"* (Hebrews 13:8) provides a resounding declaration of the divinity of Christ, timeless and unchanging, transcending the world of past, present and future, in the sphere of unending existence that belongs to God alone. Contextually, the author discards the credibility of the varied and contradictory teachings of others. By consequence, those who are not with Christ have no right to communion with His altar, that is, the Lord's Supper. Jesus died outside the gates of Jerusalem, similar to the ancient expiatory victim destroyed outside Israel's encampment in the wilderness.

At this point the readers are encouraged to unite themselves with Christ outside the religious world of contemporary Judaism, thereby sharing in the fruits of that atoning liturgy that purifies our consciences. All this goes to illustrate to them the cohesiveness and religious exclusiveness of Christianity in its own right. One cannot serve both religions anymore. The sacrifice of praise, fruit of our lips, expands the concept of priestly sacrifice, offering a precious glimpse of the sacrificial theology of the apostolic age. Sacrifice in an even further extended and spiritualized sense is to do good and to cultivate fellowship with one another. Obedience toward superiors, that is, bishops and priests, is urged. The author seems to situate himself among those leaders of the Church, and here one can even hear Paul's voice speaking in the first person.

The Letter to the Hebrews finds its epilogue and conclusion in the form of a blessing flowing into a doxology. *"Now may the God of peace who brought again from the dead our Lord Jesus, the great shepherd of the sheep, by the blood of the eternal covenant, equip you with everything good that you may do his will, working in you that which is pleasing in his sight, through Jesus Christ; to whom be glory for ever and ever. Amen"* (Hebrews 13:20–21). The only explicit reference to the Resurrection of Christ is offered here. Like the Ascension and Session, it is an integral part of the Sacrifice of Christ, the Great Shepherd of the sheep, for the ratification of the New Testament. Again in Hebrews 13:22–25 the first person singular is employed instead of the first person plural customary throughout the epistle. Interestingly, only now, at the very end the entire writing, it is qualified as a brief word of exhortation. Commentators notice the presence of Paul's companion and disciple Timothy in Hebrews 13:23, as well as the geographical identification of "Italy" in Hebrews 13:24, certainly hints that would favor a direct Pauline authorship of the letter, since they resemble a typical epistolary conclusion of Paul's other letters. Hebrews ends with a prayer for grace, sublime in its very simplicity. *"Grace be with all of you. Amen"* (Hebrews 13:25).

We live faith, not as a hypothesis, but as the certainty on which our life is based. If two people regard their love merely as a hypothesis that is constantly in need of new verification, they destroy love in that way. It is contradicted in its essence if one tries to make it something one can grasp in one's hand. By then it has already been destroyed. Perhaps so many relationships break down today because we are aware of the certainty only of the verified hypothesis and do not admit the ultimate validity of anything not scientifically proved ... Assent is produced by the will, not by the understanding's own direct insight: the particular kind of freedom of choice involved in the decision of faith rests upon this.

Joseph Cardinal Ratzinger (Pope Benedict XVI), *Pilgrim Fellowship of Faith*
(San Francisco: Ignatius Press, 2005, pp. 19–20, 23

1. Use a dictionary or your own words to define "faith." Hebrews 11:1; CCC 286

2. Compare the following passages.

Genesis 4:3–10
Hebrews 11:4

3. Explain some things about Enoch.

Genesis 5:21–24
Sirach 44:16
Sirach 49:14
Hebrews 11:5

* What do you think it means to walk with God?

4. Why is faith important?

Matthew 21:21–22
Acts 3:16
Hebrews 11:6
CCC 161

5. What is praiseworthy about Noah?

Genesis 6:13–22
Sirach 44:17–18
Hebrews 11:7

6. Why is the faith of Abraham important?

Genesis 12:1–8
Sirach 44:19–20
Hebrews 11:8–17
CCC 145

7. What enables Abraham to trust God with Isaac? Hebrews 11:17, CCC 2572

8. Describe the faith of Moses. Exodus 2:2–15; Hebrews 11:23–28

9. Who is implied in Hebrews 11:33–34? Daniel 3; 6

10. Compare the following verses:

1 King 17:17–24
Hebrews 11:35

11. What better did God have in store?

Hebrews 11:39–40
CCC 147

12. Describe the cloud of witnesses. Hebrews 12:1; CCC 1161

13. Who are witnesses of faith? Hebrews 12:1–2; CCC 165

14. Explain discipline.

Proverbs 3:11–12
Ephesians 6:4
Hebrews 12:3–11

15. List four practical instructions that you could employ from Hebrews 12:12–29.

16. Describe some biblical examples of hospitality. Hebrews 13:2

Genesis 18:1–8	
Genesis 19:1–2	
Tobit 5:9; 7:1	

* Share some times when you have offered or received hospitality.

17. What sacrament is guarded in Hebrews 13:4? CCC 1601

18. Put the advice in Hebrews 13:5 and 13:16 in your own words.

19. Give specific advice about leaders from Hebrews 13:7 and Hebrews 13:17.

20. Discuss practical ways you can bless your bishop, priest, or deacon.

Chapter 13

Letters to Churches
Revelation 1–3

"Behold, I stand at the door and knock;
if anyone hears my voice and opens the door,
I will come in to him and eat with him, and he with me."
Revelation 3:20

This last book of the New Testament canon, the Revelation to John, or the Apocalypse is perennially popular; it speaks of the last things, known as eschatology. It is thus an apocalyptic work related in style to the book of Daniel in the Old Testament. But its fascinating imagery also draws heavily on the books of Exodus and Ezekiel. John of Patmos, the author, has traditionally been identified with the writer of the Fourth Gospel and of the three letters that bear his name.

Revelation is filled with symbolism. Numbers, animals, cosmic events, colors, and names, all have a hidden symbolic meaning that can be discovered and understood by comparing them with Old Testament precedents. Because of the complexity of images and structures, the book has had the most multihued history of interpretation. Regrettably, all too often the imagery has led commentators down a smooth path of literalist interpretation that is inappropriate to the apocalyptic genre. One must keep in mind that the book is not a series of revelations (plural) but one grandiose revelation (singular, Revelation 1:1) that God will ultimately be victorious over evil. To a Church suffering severe persecution, as happened under the Roman emperor Domitian around the time of this book's origin, these words must have been soothing balm.

Using code language and symbolism derived from the Old Testament that was intended to mislead outsiders who might stumble on the book, John's Apocalypse offered struggling Christians hope in a time of tribulation. Babylon stands for the evil empire, Rome, and the beast with seven heads represents the various emperors who succeeded Domitian. The number 666 manifests the worst of evil (six falls always short of the perfect seven, and in Jewish fashion the superlative degree is expressed in triples). All of this indicates the true nature of the book—Christian apocalyptic prophecy that imparts courage and perseverance to those under persecution. The meaning, therefore, is profound yet simple, embedded in figurative details. The reader is exhorted to keep the message in this perspective and context.

The prologue (Revelation 1:1–3) introduces the author and the circumstances of the writing. Revelation was written both for the immediate future of the Apostle's own time, as well as for the two thousand years hence. Its preservation in the canon of biblical books assures us that it still has meaning today. The first major section (Revelation

1:4–3:22) consists of letters directed to the seven churches in Asia Minor, containing a message unique to each church based on their individual circumstances. Next comes a section devoted to the image of Christ as the Lamb (Revelation 4:1–5:14). This image is followed by the unsealing of various symbolic images that foretell God's ultimate victory over evil, symbolized by beasts (Revelation 6:1–20:15). After the final cosmic battle in which evil's demise is assured, a new creation with the New Jerusalem as its centerpiece emerges (Revelation 21:1–22:5). The city is without a temple, for God and the Lamb will be the only temple needed. The conclusion of the book combines testimony, prayer and hope: *"Come, Lord Jesus!"* [in Aramaic *maranatha*], (Revelation 22:20).

The Book of Revelation—Down through the ages, Revelation has been subjected to many and varied expositions and interpretations. There are five principal lines or methods of interpretation:

1) **Non-historical interpretation**—In this view, Revelation is concerned with ideas and principles, with timeless truths. Its purpose is to depict the perennial struggle of good against evil and the ultimate triumph of the kingdom of God.

2) **World (Church) historical interpretation**—In this approach, Revelation is regarded as a detailed prophecy of identifiable historical events. A variant form discerns seven stages in the history of the Church.

3) **End-historical interpretation**—Revelation is taken to be exclusively concerned with the happenings at the close of the age that will usher in the Second Coming of Christ.

4) **Contemporary-historical interpretation**—This method presupposes that Revelation is wholly concerned with the circumstances of John's day. Thus the book is warning the Christians of the persecution to come upon them and has no relevance to later ages.

5) **Mystical interpretation**—Revelation is understood as a portrayal of the way the individual soul seeks union with Christ.

John's symbolism—John's highly figurative language includes anthropological (human), cosmic (cataclysmic), theriomorphic (animals), chromatic (colors), and arithmetic (numbers express quality, not numerical quantity), symbols. The author uses symbols cumulatively, soliciting the reader to interpret them individually.

Colors: White = Joy, victory, sharing in Christ's Resurrection.
Green = Death.
Black = Disaster.
Red   = Blood, martyrdom.
Gold   = Eternity, divinity, royalty.

Numbers are interpreted along the following parameters:

- 1 = Unity, referring to God.
- 3 = The Trinity (omne trinum est perfectum).
- 4 = Creation (4 corners of the earth); Nature (4 seasons).
- 6 = Imperfection (7 − 1).
- 7 = 3 + 4 = Perfection, Totality, Salvation. God and creation reunited.
- 8 = Regeneration; the number of beatitudes.
- 9 = Mystery (3 x 3).
- 10 = Worldly power, the limited time of the world, and historical completion.
- 12 = God's people (3 x 4).
- 40 = The Church's tests and trials (10 x 4).
- 144,000 = 12 Tribes of Israel x 12 Apostles x 1000 = God's people, His Church.

The Apocalypse of Jesus Christ (Revelation 1:1–8)—"Apocalypse" means unveiling, a revelation. Jesus Christ is at the same time the Revealer and the Revelation, revealing Himself as the center of world history (Ephesians 1:2–14). The verb "to show" here, literally means "explain by signs" (Greek *semainein*). The message lays concealed in the visionary images. God's servants are the prophets of the era of the Church, and they are the recipients of this revelation (Revelation 10:7; 11:18; 22:6; also Amos 3:7). *"What must soon take place"* (Revelation 1:1) is God's providence and design of salvation. The angels, an important feature of apocalyptic literature, are spiritual guides who interpret the heavenly visions.

There are many spiritual powers, to whom the name *angels* is given ... There are, according to John, angels of the Churches in Asia ... And, as the Lord teaches, there are for little children, angels who see God daily. There are, as Raphael told Tobias, angels assisting before the majesty of God, and carrying to God the prayers of suppliants. Mention is made of all this, because you might wish to understand those angels as the eyes, or the ears, or the hands, or the feet of God ... It is not the nature of God, but the weakness of men, which requires their service. For they are sent for the sake of those who will inherit salvation.

(Saint Hilary of Poitiers [315–368 AD], *Commentaries on the Psalms*, 129, 7)

Saint John is described as a witness for Christ, someone who publicly proclaims the truth (Isaiah 43:10–12; 44:8; Acts 1:8, 22; 2:32; 10:39ff; 22:20), and seals his confession with blood (Revelation 2:13; 11:3; 17:6; 18:24). The first of seven Beatitudes (Revelation 1:3; 14:13; 16:15; 19:9; 20:6; 22:7, 14) refers to the reading of this prophecy in liturgical assemblies, most especially the Eucharist.

The greeting and benediction provide a veritable tapestry of Old Testament passages (Psalm 89; Isaiah 54–55; Daniel 7; Zechariah 12), focusing on the all-embracing Kingship of the Messiah reigning over the people of God by virtue of the promises made to his ancestor David. Since "seven" conveys fullness, the "seven churches" really symbolize the whole Church in Asia Minor. "Grace and Peace" is a combination of the customary Hellenistic (*chairein* = grace) and Oriental (*shalom* = peace) greetings, characterizing the entire Christ-event. Saint John then identifies God the Father with the God of Exodus, revealed to Moses in the burning bush (Exodus 3:14). "The seven spirits before the throne" illustrate the fullness of the Holy Spirit in Christ and in His Church. Drawing on Isaiah 55:4 and Psalm 89:27, He is described as *"Jesus Christ the faithful witness"* (Revelation 1:5). With Jesus, the "Firstborn" (1 Corinthians 15:20; Colossians 1:18) the resurrection from the dead is initiated. Daniel 7:14 inspires the expression "ruler of kings on earth."

The text flows into a doxology. "... *Jesus Christ the faithful witness, the first-born of the dead, and the ruler of kings on earth. To him who loves us and has freed us from our sins by his blood and made us a kingdom, priests to his God and Father, to him be glory and dominion for ever and ever. Amen"* (Revelation 1:5–6). Here, the sacred author uses originality and recall of Exodus 19:6 to merge royal and priestly dignity bestowed on God's people, who will be united to Christ the High Priest (Letter to the Hebrews). They offer themselves as well as the universe in a sacrifice of praise. Daniel 7:13 and Zechariah 12:10 are combined: *"Behold, he is coming with the clouds, and every eye will see him, every one who pierced him; and all tribes of the earth will wail on account of him"* (Revelation 1:7) to communicate that He who has been put to death by man will return as the divinely appointed Judge of all (Mark 14:62), and His adversaries' repentance will come too late. "Pantocrator" (All-Ruler, the Almighty) applies here to God the Father (later in Revelation 22:13, referring to the Son). These opening verses of the book are remarkably expressive and rich in dogma, pointing to the Blessed Trinity, the Incarnation and Redemption in Christ, His Church and the Last Judgment. The "Alpha and Omega" is the only valid key to understand history.

Inaugural vision of the Son of Man (Revelation 1:9–20)—John is on Patmos, an island of banishment from the Roman Empire, sharing in the tribulations of the Church like a brother. In the Spirit on the Day of the Lord, John hears a voice like a trumpet (like on Sinai, Exodus 19:16) with a message for seven cities. Christ appears to him *"One like a Son of Man"* (Revelation 1:13) reminiscent of Daniel 7:13; 10:6, active in the Church, symbolized by the lampstands. His ankle-length robe signifies His *priesthood* (Exodus 28:4; 29:5; Zechariah 3:4), His *kingship* is represented by a golden sash (1 Maccabees 10:89; 11:58), His eternity by white hair (Daniel 7:9), His omniscience by the blazing eyes, His omnipotence and immutability by feet like burnished bronze (Daniel 2:31–35; 10:6), and His *prophetic* stature by the oceanic voice and sharp two-edged sword issuing from His mouth (Revelation 19:15ff). Saint John had fallen at His feet and the Lord of History touches him like He had done on Tabor (Matthew 17:7), readying him to receive and transmit hidden things of present and future. The mystery of the seven stars and seven golden lampstands is revealed in that they symbolize the seven churches and their angels (bishops or guardian angels). Again, the seven churches represent the whole Church of all times confronted with ungodliness. This official interpretation helps the reader understand that all the images still to come have a deeper meaning as well, to be retrieved by the help of Old Testament precedents.

Letter to Ephesus (Revelation 2:1–7)—Ephesus was the capital of Asia Minor, seat of early emperor worship. Christianity was brought here by Saint Paul (Acts 18:23–21:16) and later on Saint Timothy was its bishop. Where the goddess Artemis was once worshiped, here the Blessed Virgin Mary was proclaimed as (*Theotokos* in Greek), the Mother of God (Council of Ephesus, 431). Christ is actively present to His Church always menaced by false prophets. *"I know you are enduring patiently and bearing up for my name's sake, and you have not grown weary. But I have this against you, that you have abandoned the love you had at first"* (Revelation 2:3–4). Sadly, one's first love can be abandoned, and only true repentance achieves conversion. Christ owns the Spirit in fullness and through Him guides the Church (2 Corinthians 3:17). Victory is promised with language borrowed from Genesis 2:9; 3:22 and from Wisdom texts (Proverbs 3:18; 13:12; 15:4). The reward is one and the same: a share in the eternal reign of Christ!

Letter to Smyrna (Revelation 2:8–11)—This pagan city excelled in its loyalty to Rome, and tradition holds that Paul founded the Church there. Smyrna also had an influential Jewish community. Christ is again identified as the first and the last, the Alpha and the Omega. Whoever does not welcome the preaching of the Apostles in the New Israel of the Church must be called an opponent, the *"synagogue of Satan"* (Revelation 2:9). Christians are encouraged to endure a brief period of trial—*"ten days"* (Genesis 24:55; Daniel 1:14)—in order to receive the *"crown of life"* (2 Timothy 4:8; 1 Peter 5:4). *"He who conquers shall not be hurt by the second death"* (Revelation 2:11), that is, spiritual and eternal death.

Letter to Pergamum (Revelation 2:12–17)—Pergamum, a center of all forms of paganism, including a thriving emperor cult, receives a prophecy from *"Him who has the sharp two-edged sword"* (Revelation 2:12). Unfortunately, nothing is known of the Antipas mentioned here. There is a Jewish tradition about Balaam (Numbers 22–24; 31:16; 2 Peter 2:15; Jude 11) advising the Moabite women to give themselves to the Israelites on condition that the Jews accept their foreign gods and take part in their pagan sacrifices (Numbers 25:1). In biblical language, falling away from the One True God was considered a form of adultery (idolatry equals immorality). Moreover, some see the Nicolatians as a sect originating in the apostasy of one of the seven deacons mentioned in Acts 6:5, maybe a Jewish-Gnostic movement. They appear to have been infiltrators and pseudo-prophets out to undermine the purity of Christian faith in Pergamum. But all those who repent will receive the hidden Manna, a figure for eternal life (John 6; Hebrews 9:4). According to rabbinical teaching, at the end of time manna was to come down from heaven and feed the faithful. Lastly, the white stone with a new name may point to the little pebbles that the ancients used as tickets to enter one of their stadiums or theaters. White in apocalyptic literature signals joy, purity, victory and life. The new name symbolizes the New Creation of heaven.

Letter to Thyatira (Revelation 2:18–29)—Thyatira, a military outpost, was well-known for its workers' guild (Acts 16:14) involving pagan worship. A modern Jezebel (1 Kings 16:31ff; 2 Kings 9:22–30ff) claims to be a prophetess but leads the population into idolatry. Perhaps the Thyatirans believed that one must experience the depth of

Satanic power to be liberated from it. But to the victor is given a share in the kingdom, the "rod of iron" (Psalm 2:8; Revelation 12:5; 19:15). Jesus calls Himself the morning star, an oriental image for power and dominion. It may well include the notion of Resurrection and Ascension (Acts 2:32–36; Philippians 2:9–11; 2 Peter 1:19; and the *Exultet* of the Easter Vigil).

Letter to Sardis (Revelation 3:1–6)—Sardis, a city proverbial for its wealth in the sixth century BC, was a contemporary provincial city, and a center of wool manufacturing. The caution to be vigilant may be based on its repeated defeat by enemies. When the visionary of Patmos wrote to this Christian community, it was alive in name only but not in spirit. This spiritual sleep and the figure of a thief is amply illustrated in Matthew 24:43; Luke 15:24; Romans 6:13; 13:11; 1 Thessalonians 5:2–6; and 2 Peter 3:10. Invariably these letters end in a final promise of eternal life, here under the symbol of a "white garment" (Revelation 4:4; 6:11; 7:9) and "the book of life" (Revelation 20:12).

Letter to Philadelphia (Revelation 3:7–13)—Philadelphia had been utterly destroyed by an earthquake in 17 AD and rebuilt under the name Flavia, hence the "pillars" and "name." Christ the Messiah identifies Himself symbolically as the *"key of David"* (Isaiah 22:22). Jesus is able to open the door for successful evangelization (see also Acts 14:26ff; 1 Corinthians 16:9; 2 Corinthians 2:12; Colossians 4:3) as well as ultimately to His kingdom. Although Saint Ignatius remembers trouble with Judaizing Christians, any individual or group that rejects or opposes Jesus' love can be qualified as the *"synagogue of Satan"* (Hebrews 3:9). Of this one can be assured, God will come "soon" and intervene. Eventually, those who are saved will bear three names as a sign of property: God's, the City's, and Christ's (Numbers 6:27).

Letter to Laodicea (Revelation 3:14–22)—Laodicea was an industrial center for woolen garments and ointments, with a flourishing medical academy, having mineral springs and white cliffs in its vicinity. Laodicea was also razed by an earthquake but soon rebuilt. At the beginning of His message to this local Church Jesus calls Himself the Amen, stressing His divine trustworthiness. He is the Incarnate *"God of Truth"* (Isaiah 65:16), the flawless "Yes" to His Father's will. By mentioning creation, a link is established with Wisdom, Proverbs 8:22; Wisdom 9:1; 1 Corinthians 8:6; Colossians 1:16; Hebrews 1:3; and John 1:3. One must have an undivided and unconditional dedication to His Church, avoiding all tepidity (allusion to hot springs nearby). False riches and spiritual blindness are denounced. But the one who opens himself up to the Lord's gracious presence will enjoy the messianic fullness, presented under the figure of a common meal. The table fellowship in the orient expressed union and harmony as well as obligation. In the scriptures it becomes a symbol of Christ's lavish gifts to us (Isaiah 25:6; Song of Solomon 5:1; Matthew 8:11; 22:12; 25:10; Luke 22:29ff). God speaks to the people of the early Church and continues to issue an invitation to people today to open the door of their hearts to Him and give Him their first love.

The Lord knocks again and again at the door of the human heart. In the Book of Revelation he says to the "angel" of the Church of Laodicea and, through him, to the people of all times: *Behold, I stand at the door and knock; if any one hears my voice and opens the door, I will come in to him and eat with him, and he with me"* (Revelation 3:20). The Lord is at the door—at the door of the world and at the door of every individual heart. He knocks to be let in: the Incarnation of God, his taking flesh, must continue until the end of time. All must be reunited in Christ in one body: the great hymns on Christ in the Letters to the Ephesians and to the Colossians tell us this. Christ knocks. Today too He needs people who, so to speak, make their own flesh available to Him, give Him the matter of the world and of their lives, thus serving the unification between God and the world, until the reconciliation of the universe. Dear friends, it is your task to knock at people's hearts in Christ's Name. By entering into union with Christ yourselves, you will also be able to assume Gabriel's role: to bring Christ's call to men.

(Pope Benedict XVI, *Homily of His Holiness,* September 29, 2007)

1. Complete the following beatitudes found in Revelation:

Blessed is he who reads aloud the words of the prophecy, and blessed are those who hear, and who keep what is written therein.	Revelation 1:3
Blessed are the dead who die in the Lord.	Revelation 14:13
	Revelation 16:15
	Revelation 19:9
	Revelation 20:6
	Revelation 22:7
	Revelation 22:14

2. What will happen when Jesus comes again in glory?

Zechariah 12:10
Matthew 24:29–31 or Mark 14:62
Revelation 1:7

3. How has God revealed Himself? Exodus 3:14; Revelation 1:4–8

4. Find a common description in the following verses:

Isaiah 43:10–12; 44:6–8
Acts 1:8, 22; 2:32; 10:39
Revelation 1:1–2

* When have you been a witness for Christ?

5. Why do we pray for peace? Revelation 1:4; CCC 2854

6. Explain some things that Jesus does.

Revelation 1:5–6
CCC 1546

7. Describe who John saw.

Daniel 7:13–14; 10:5–6
Revelation 1:12–16

8. What common emotion and gesture appears in the following passages?

Isaiah 44:2
Matthew 17:7
Revelation 1:17

* Recall a time when God comforted you in your fear or confusion.

9. What does "Alpha and Omega" mean? Revelation 1:8; 1:17b

10. What happened after Jesus died?

Revelation 1:18
CCC 633, 645

11. Who received this vision, and where was he? Revelation 1:9

12. Summarize the message to Ephesus. Revelation 2:2–7

13. Explain some aspects of the human heart and human tears.

Revelation 2:4–5
CCC 401, 1429

14. What common thing can you find in these verses? Genesis 2:9; Revelation 2:7b

15. What can we expect to receive in heaven?

Revelation 2:17
CCC 1025, 2159

16. Summarize the messages to the Churches in these cities:

Smyrna	Revelation 2:8–11
Pergamum	Revelation 2:12–17
Thyatira	Revelation 2:18–29

17. Who initiates and ultimately controls human events? Revelation 3:7; CCC 303

18. Summarize the messages to the Churches in these cities:

Sardis	Revelation 3:1–6
Philadelphia	Revelation 3:7–13
Laodicea	Revelation 3:14–22

* Explain lukewarmness (Revelation 3:15–16). What does it look like in you?

19. Who is the "Amen" in Revelation 3:14? CCC 1065

20. Describe the invitation issued in Revelation 3:20. *How should you respond?

Chapter 14
Heavenly Worship
Revelation 4–5

"Worthy is the Lamb who was slain, to receive power and wealth and wisdom and might and honor and glory and blessing!"
And I heard every creature in heaven and on earth
and under the earth and in the sea, and all therein, saying,
"To him who sits upon the throne and to the Lamb
be blessing and honor and glory and might for ever and ever!"
Revelation 5:12–13

Eternal worship (**Revelation 4:1–11**)—Each of the foregoing letters may have been attached individually like a cover letter to the prophecy contained in Revelation 4:1–22:21. Chapters 4 and 5 function as the backdrop against which the drama is unfolding and to which the visionary on Patmos constantly refers (Revelation 7:11; 11:16; 14:3; 19:4; 20:11; 21:5). John is masterfully drawing especially on Ezekiel 1:10 to depict the eternal worship of God by all creation, but also on Daniel 7:9 and Isaiah 61:1ff. The expression *"I looked, and behold in heaven an open door"* (Revelation 4:1) is characteristic of apocalyptic writings. Heaven is understood as a solid vault with doors that give access to it (Isaiah 64:1; Mark 1:10; Acts 7:56). Saint John sees the earth from heaven's vantage point. Ezekiel 1:26 and 10:1 explain the images in heaven. The rainbow indicates divine reconciliation and peace (Genesis 9:12–17). *"God is light and in him is no darkness"* (1 John 1:5). The striking feature of the throne in heaven is a fundamental theme of the book: its majesty will stand out in contrast to other thrones.

"Round the throne were twenty-four thrones, and seated on the thrones were twenty-four elders, clothed in white garments, with golden crowns upon their heads" (Revelation 4:4). These may represent (a) the twenty-four classes of priests, 1 Chronicles 24:1–9, (b) the twelve patriarchs or tribes of Jacob and the twelve apostles as a prototype of the Church, (c) the angels, Matthew 18:10; Tobit 12:12, (d) the Old and the New Law of God, or (e) simply the heavenly court, Isaiah 24:23. They are figuratively partaking in Christ's Resurrection (white garments) and victorious kingdom (golden crowns). *"From the throne issue flashes of lightning and peals of thunder"* (Revelation 4:5) recall regular companions of divine apparitions in the Old Testament theophanies (Exodus 19:16; Ezekiel 1:13; Zechariah 4:2). Are the "seven flaming torches" akin to the seven spirits in Revelation 1:4; 3:1; 5:6? Some maintain that these are the "angels of the Countenance" and belong to the highest rank in the angelic hierarchy as archangels (Tobit 12:15), reflecting the fullness of divine fire. Not so easy to clarify is the image of the *"sea of glass like crystal"* (Revelation 4:6a). A similar appearance in Exodus 24:10 helps the reader to see John's throne vision in the light of the God of the Exodus, of deliverance, of Sinai's Torah and Wisdom, of the blood of the Covenant, and of communion with

the Divine. Moses, Aaron, Nadab, and Abihu beheld God, and ate and drank (Exodus 24). Psalm 104:3 sings: *"Who have laid the beams of your chambers upon the waters"* like heavenly furnishings.

Next, the Apostle is riveted by the sight of four living creatures (Revelation 4:6b–8a), reflecting the picture found in Ezekiel 1:4–21, although with slightly differing details. Symbolically speaking, they reveal the highest attributes of the visible and invisible world—the number four is the apocalyptic symbol for cosmos—before the throne of the Almighty. His glory is manifested in nobility (lion), wisdom (man), power (ox), and swiftness (eagle). Indeed, these magnificent qualities are God's in an infinite degree, and the living creatures' many eyes makes us glimpse God's own omniscience and providence. Saint Irenaeus is the first of the Patristic era to apply these to the four Evangelists (Matthew–man; Mark–lion; Luke–ox; John–eagle). Matthew's Gospel begins with the genealogy of Jesus, the man. Mark's Gospel begins in the wilderness, where lions live. Luke's Gospel includes the infancy narrative of Jesus, born in the manger, where the ox would dwell. John's Gospel provides theological insights about Christ's divinity that soar like an eagle.

> The lion is the king of beasts. Our Savior, the King of Kings, is called a lion because of His power, the strength by which He conquered the devil in death. But why is He called the whelp of a lion, when elsewhere He is called the conqueror from the tribe of Judah? He is called a whelp to show that it refers not to the Father, but to the Son of God. For when both a lion and a whelp of a lion are named, both the Father and the Son are indicated. Their nature is not divided, but distinct Persons are manifested. For just as a lion is born of a lion, so too it is said that God proceeds from God, and Light from Light. And just as there is no change of nature when a lion is born of a lion, and a single origin is manifested, so also God is born of God, and cannot be other than God.
>
> (Saint Gregory of Elvira, [†392 AD], *Homilies on Sacred Scripture*, 6)

"Holy, holy, holy, is the Lord God Almighty, who was and is and is to come! …Worthy are you, our Lord and God, to receive glory and honor and power, for you created all things, and by your will they existed and were created" (Revelation 4:8b, 11) records their eternal praises in the form of a doxology which has its roots in Isaiah 6:2ff and Psalm 47:6–8. The ultimate purpose of all Creation is to praise its Maker, Lord and King. By casting their crowns before the throne, they acknowledge His universal sovereignty forever. Compare the hymns of Revelation (Revelation 5:9–10) to see the way they reassure us concerning God's final victory, and how world history is unfolding within the all-encompassing reality of the cosmic liturgy celebrated before His throne. Revelation 4 highlights God as Creator, whereas Chapter 5 shows Him to be our Savior.

The scroll and the Lamb (Revelation 5:1–14)—*"And I saw in the right hand of him who was seated on the throne a scroll written within and on the back, sealed with seven* *seals"*(Revelation 5:1). This vision is closely related to the same reality in Ezekiel 2:9. In the ancient orient a document drawn up on clay or papyrus was at times fitted with a cover and the same message repeated on the other side to guard against falsification. A ribbon was then passed around the scroll and it was sealed. The "seven seals" here emphasize the extreme importance and confidentiality of the message, which contains God's design for all of humanity for all times, the *Theology of History*, as it were, until the Lamb's epic victory over the Dragon is completed, and the Lord comes again. The eventual breaking of the seals, signals the accomplishment of His plan of salvation, and it is the Messiah Himself who makes it known and understandable. He is the "Lion from the tribe of Judah" (Genesis 49:9), the "Root of David" (Isaiah 11:1), and the "Root of Jesse raised up to govern the Gentiles" (Romans 15:12). Paradoxically, the seer weeps, expressing humanity's dilemma and incapacity of deciphering its own history.

At last a champion is found as the focus now shifts to the Lamb. *"I saw a Lamb standing, as though it had been slain"* (Revelation 5:6). The reader must take each aspect of this symbolism of the Apocalypse and interpret it individually, before putting the whole message together at the end. First, the Lamb is a peculiarly Christian title for Christ recalling the Passover lamb (Exodus 12:21–27), as well as the innocent Lamb of the Servant of God (Isaiah 53:7). The Lamb is described in John 1:29–36; Acts 8:32; Hebrews 9:14; and 1 Peter 1:19. Its state of being "slain" indicates Jesus' Passion and Death. He is paradoxically "standing" at the same time in His Resurrection, "dead and alive" (Revelation 1:18; Hebrews 7:25). The "seven horns" are a sign of Christ's infinite power, and its "seven eyes" mean the indwelling of the Holy Spirit that pervades the whole world (Revelation 1:4; 3:1; 4:5; Zechariah 4:10). Eloquently, in Revelation 1:4 the seven spirits belong to the Father, here they belong to the Lamb. Its position is the absolute center of the kingdom "throne," surrounded by the living beings and the elders. This Lamb now has the right to break open the seals of the scroll because of its victory over Satan by His Paschal mystery, being Lion and Lamb at the same time.

The angels and the whole creation sing another hymn of praise for the redemptive work of the Lamb. *"Worthy are you to take the scroll and to open its seals, for you were slain and by your blood you ransomed men for God from every tribe and tongue and people and nation, and have made them a kingdom and priests to our God, and they shall reign on earth ... Worthy is the Lamb who was slain to receive power and wealth and wisdom and might and honor and glory and blessing! To him who sits upon the throne and to the Lamb be blessing and honor and glory and might for ever and ever!"* (Revelation 5:9–10, 12–13). The chant is new because of the amazing and never-aging novelty of the gift of salvation. The original Covenant with Israel (Exodus 19; 24:4–11) was ratified in blood (Genesis 9:6; Leviticus 7:26f; 17:11; Deuteronomy 12:23). This hymn exults in the creation of a people that is at the same time priestly and royal, totally God's possession. This dazzling and profoundly reassuring vision of an uninterrupted cosmic liturgy now sets the stage for the first act of the dramatic confrontation between the *eschatological* (biblical Greek for "end-time") forces of good and evil.

The subject of the Resurrection on which we reflected last week unfolds a new perspective, that of the expectation of the Lord's return. It thus brings us to ponder on the relationship among the present time, the time of the Church and of the Kingdom of Christ, and the future *(éschaton)* that lies in store for us, when Christ will consign the Kingdom to his Father. Every Christian discussion of the last things, called eschatology, always starts with the event of the Resurrection; in this event the last things have already begun and, in a certain sense, are already present.

... Paul describes Christ's *parousia* [Second Coming Glory] in especially vivid tones and with symbolic imagery which, however, conveys a simple and profound message: we shall ultimately be with the Lord for ever ... As believers, we are already with the Lord in our lifetime; our future, eternal life, has already begun...

After examining the various aspects of the expectation of Christ's parousia, let us ask ourselves: what are the basic convictions of Christians as regards the last things: death, the end of the world? Their first conviction is the certainty that Jesus is Risen and is with the Father and thus is with us forever. And no one is stronger than Christ, for he is with the Father, he is with us. We are consequently safe, free of fear ... Christ lives, he has overcome death, he has overcome all these powers. We live in this certainty, in this freedom, and in this joy. This is the first aspect of our living with regard to the future.

The second is the certainty that Christ is with me. And just as the future world in Christ has already begun, this also provides the certainty of hope. The future is not darkness in which no one can find his way. It is not like this. Without Christ, even today the world's future is dark, and fear of the future is so common. Christians know that Christ's light is stronger and therefore they live with a hope that is not vague, with a hope that gives them certainty and courage to face the future.

Lastly, their third conviction is that the Judge who returns at the same time as Judge and Savior has left us the duty to live in this world in accordance with his way of living ... Our third conviction, therefore, is responsibility before Christ for the world, for our brethren and at the same time also for the certainty of his mercy.

... Finally, a last point that might seem to us somewhat difficult. At the end of his First Letter to the Corinthians, Saint Paul reiterates and also puts on the lips of the Corinthians a prayer that originated in the first Christian communities in the Palestinian area: *Maraná thá!* which means literally, "Our Lord, come!" It was the prayer of early Christianity and also of the last book of the New Testament, Revelation, which ends with it: "Come, Lord Jesus!" Can we pray like this too?

Pope Benedict XVI, *General Audience,* November 12, 2008

We thank you, holy Father, for your holy name, which you have caused to dwell in our hearts; and for the knowledge and faith and immortality which you have made known to us through Jesus your Son. Glory be to you forever. You, almighty Master, have created all things for your name's sake, and have given food and drink to men for their enjoyment, so that they might return thanks to you. Upon us, however, you have bestowed spiritual food and drink, and eternal life through your Servant. Above all we give you thanks, because you are mighty. Glory be to you forever.

Remember, O Lord, your Church. Deliver it from every evil and perfect it in your love. Gather it from the four winds, sanctified for your kingdom, which you have prepared for it. For yours is the power and the glory forever. Let grace come, and let this world pass away. Hosanna to the God of David. If anyone is holy, let him come; if anyone is not, let him repent. *Marana tha.*

(Didache or *Teaching of the Apostles,* [140 AD], 10, 1)

1. Compare the following passages:

Exodus 19:16
Revelation 4:1

2. What sights and sounds would you expect to find in heaven?

Ezekiel 1:26–28
Zachariah 4:2
Revelation 4:1–8

* Who and what would you expect to find in heaven?

3. Describe the heavenly liturgy and those who participate in it.

Revelation 4:2–11
CCC 1138
CCC 1139
CCC 2642

4. Describe the twenty-four elders. Revelation 4:4

5. What can you learn about the four living creatures?

Ezekiel 1:4–25
Revelation 4:6–8

6. Identify four living creatures and compare to the four Evangelists. Ezekiel 1:10

Revelation 4:7	*Man*	*Matthew*
	Lion	

7. When do you sing part of the verse in Revelation 4:8?

8. Compare the following verses:

Psalm 47:1–3
Revelation 4:8–9

9. Why did God create the world?

Revelation 4:11
CCC 295

10. How do the twenty-four elders worship? Revelation 4:10–11

* How do you worship God?

11. What special thing can God do?

Romans 4:17
Revelation 4:11

12. What can you learn from the following verses?

Isaiah 29:11
Ezekiel 2:9–10
Revelation 5:1

13. Who can you identify from the following verses?

Genesis 49:8–10
Revelation 5:5

14. Describe the Lamb.

Exodus 12:21–27
Isaiah 53:7
John 1:29–36
1 Peter 1:18–19
Revelation 5:6

* When and how do you pray to the Lamb of God? Do you know it in Latin?

15. What did the twenty-four elders do before the Lamb? Revelation 5:8

16. What were the elders holding? Revelation 5:8

17. What does God do for His people?

Exodus 19:6
Revelation 5:10

18. What does Jesus do for us? Revelation 5:10; CCC 1544

19. How many angels prayed around the throne? Revelation 5:11

20. Memorize one of the prayers in Revelation 4–5, or write one of your own.

Monthly Social Activity

This month, your small group will meet for coffee, tea, or a simple breakfast, lunch, or dessert in someone's home. Pray for this social event and for the host or hostess. Try, if at all possible, to attend.

After a short prayer and some time for small talk, share about a time that you had an especially heavenly worship experience. Perhaps it was a Mass one Christmas or Easter or Pentecost. Or it may have been a retreat experience or a prayer time or prayer meeting. Make sure that everyone has time to share.

Examples

◆ *One Christmas, my children were in the pageant at the Children's Mass. My parents and grandmother were in Mass. It was snowing outside and we were singing carols. I treasure that moment forever.*

◆ *One year I had an especially meaningful Lent. After I had fasted and prayed during Lent, I felt incredible joy at the Easter vigil Mass.*

◆ *Last year, for Pentecost, I went back to my old parish. The music was outstanding; the preaching was inspired. It felt as if the roof would open and we could worship with all of the angels and saints in heaven.*

Chapter 15
Seals and Trumpets
Revelation 6–8

"For the Lamb in the midst of the throne will be their shepherd,
and he will guide them to springs of living water;
and God will wipe away every tear from their eyes."
Revelation 7:17

The first four seals: four horsemen (Revelation 6:1–8)—The language of this chapter is quite parallel to the eschatological speeches of Christ in the Synoptic Gospels, (Matthew 24:1–35; Mark 13:1–31; Luke 21:5–33). There is also considerable affinity with Zechariah 1:8–10 and 6:1–8. Generally, the threats of scourge by war, hunger, plague, and wild beasts can be found often on the lips of the prophets (Ezekiel 6:11ff; 7:15; 12:16; Jeremiah 14:12; 15:2). The main thought of the Apostle is to characterize by means of Old Testament figures the history of the people of God marked by persecution and tribulation at all times.

Thus, the *first* rider on a white horse does not represent Christ, as he does in Revelation 19:11–13, or the victorious campaign of the Good News in the world. Here the rider stands for an invading power that anonymously undermines the security of the earthly society. The *second* rider, emerging on a red horse is a symbol of war (Mark 13:8). As the *third* seal is opened, a black horse appears, which together with the scale and prohibitive prices (a minimal ration of cheap flour for a day's wage) indicates food shortage and famine (see Ezekiel 4:16). "Oil and wine" could point to the preservation of staple products, or can represent those who will be spared because of the liturgical association. The *fourth* horse is given a name, "death" and Hades (netherworld) clings to it (Revelation 1:18; 20:13ff). Christ, however, holds the keys to both.

When the *fifth* seal opens, the martyrs cry for redress. They are found under the altar (Revelation 11:1). They turn to God for vindication, to show Himself faithful to His promises regarding the victory of saints, those in white robes. This implies the judgment of the world (Psalm 79, Zechariah 1:12; John 12:48; 16:11–33; Matthew 23:37–39). In the Jerusalem temple the blood of animals was regularly poured at the foot of the altar, symbolizing life. The martyrs of the Old Testament are longing, too, for the coming of God's kingdom. This episode may have provided the rationale for the practice of preserving relics of saints under the altars of our Catholic churches.

On the occasion of the breaking of the *sixth* seal, the reader is confronted with a cosmic upheaval described with a whole array of apocalyptic imagery. These cosmic signs are part of a prophetic tradition announcing the unleashing of divine judgment from which nobody can escape. Their mention here also emphasizes the end of an era and the ushering in of a new era, prefacing the great eschatological drama to come (Isaiah 2:10–19; 13:10; 34:4; Jeremiah 4:24; Amos 8:8f; Joel 2:31; Nahum 1:3ff; Hosea 10:8). Through Judaism and its trials, the messianic era is born (Isaiah 13; Nahum 1–3). As a proof for the symbolic value of this cosmic imagery one has to remember how Saint Peter quotes the Minor Prophet Joel on the very day of Pentecost *"And it shall come to pass afterward, that I will pour out my spirit on all flesh"* (Joel 2:28–32; Acts 2:17–21), showing how Joel's predictions all refer to the mighty and irresistible irruption of the divine Spirit into the world that day. Thus, any literal reading of these traditional images throughout Revelation risks missing the point.

Interlude: The sealing of the elect (Revelation 7:1–17)—Behind the image of "four world corners" lies the idea of the ancients that our planet was flat and cornered (Ezekiel 7:2; 37:9). The "four winds and angels" are seen as stewards of creation (Revelation 14:18; 16:5; Zechariah 6:5; Daniel 7:2). Indeed, it was a Jewish notion that mild winds originated from the four sides, destructive winds from the four corners. *"Do not harm the earth or the sea or the trees, till we have sealed the servants of our God upon their foreheads"* (Revelation 7:3) has a notable precedent in Ezekiel 9 and Exodus 12. Those sealed with the Hebrew *tau* or with the blood of the Lamb belong to the Lord. They will be protected until the end even with supernatural strength, although they may still suffer physical harm and pestilence (Revelation 9:4; 14:1; 22:4).

The number of those sealed is 144,000 = 12 times 12 times 1000. This number is not intended to be a literal, mathematical number, but rather signifies a great multitude, distinct from those who follow the Beast. This seal alludes to the indelible mark that is impressed on those who receive the Sacraments of Baptism, Confirmation and Holy Orders. Numbers play a prominent role in the apocalyptic literary genre. They do not stand for quantity, but rather for quality. If they can be reduced to the factors of three or four they represent a good and redeemed reality. Here we see the new and true Israel, the Church, the community of the elect of God at any moment in history (James 1:1; Galatians 6:16), not excluding the saints of the Old Covenant. The list of the tribes of Israel is unconventional. Judah is listed first, perhaps because it is the messianic tribe. Manasseh replaces Dan, probably due to the Rabbinic tradition that the antichrist would come from Dan.

A most encouraging vision emerges. *"These are they who have come out of the great tribulation; they have washed their robes and made them white in the blood of the Lamb"* (Revelation 7:14), echoing Daniel 12:1. They owe their spiritual bliss to the blood of the Lamb. A literary device introduces the message with great impact. Furthermore, *"the Word became flesh and dwelt among us"* (John 1:14) reinforces the idea of God pitching His tent among His beloved people, just as He had done in the wilderness. *"Therefore are they before the throne of God, and serve him day and night within his temple; and he who sits upon the throne will shelter them with his presence"* (Revelation 7:15) neatly prepares for the even more complete portrayal of heaven in Revelation 21. John the Apostle was inspired by Isaiah *"they shall not hunger or thirst"* (Isaiah 49:10) when he wrote *"they shall hunger no more, neither thirst any more; the sun shall not strike them, nor any scorching heat*" (Revelation 7:16). He describes the Lamb that shepherds the sheep, reminiscent of Psalm 23. "*God will wipe away every tear from their eyes*" (Revelation 7:17) recalls Isaiah 25:8.

Great silence in heaven precedes the seven trumpets (Revelation 8:1–13)—As a solemn prelude to the ever-increasing cataclysms the *seventh* seal causes silence in heaven. A pregnant pause forces a waiting period of uncertainty and anticipation. "*I am Raphael, one of the seven holy angels who present the prayers of the saints and enter into the presence of the glory of the Lord*" (Tobit 12:15) prefigures this vision. "*Then I saw the seven angels who stand before God, and seven trumpets were given to them*" (Revelation 8:2). Trumpets in the Old Testament herald divine intervention and guidance, they also announce and accompany festivals and warfare (Exodus 19:16; Isaiah 27:13; Joel 2:1; Zechariah 9:14). In the New Testament trumpets become signs of Christ's Parousia, His Second Coming in Glory (1 Corinthians 15:52; 1 Thessalonians 4:16; Matthew 24:31). The comforting presence of the angels are designed to encourage the suffering people of God, assuring them that their prayers reach the throne of God and are heard (Psalm 141:2). The angel takes the charcoals and scatters them on the earth, causing thunder and earthquake, harbingers of God's impending judgment.

The first four trumpets form a unity. Moses' plagues in Egypt provide a prototype and literary background. Old Testament events from Exodus and Jeremiah prefigure the catastrophic events released by the angels in Revelation.

Hail was the seventh plague in Egypt. (Exodus 9:24–26)	The first angel blew his trumpet, and *hail* and fire mixed with blood fell on the earth. (Revelation 8:7)
In the first plague of Egypt, the Nile River was turned into *blood*. (Exodus 7:20–24)	A third of the sea became *blood*. (Revelation 8:9)
God fed his people with *wormwood* and made them drink *poisonous water*. (Jeremiah 9:15)	The waters became *wormwood*, and many died of *bitter water*. (Revelation 8:11)
Moses caused thick *darkness* to fall as the ninth plague of Egypt. (Exodus 10:22)	The sun, moon and stars were struck and there was *darkness*. (Revelation 8:12)

"A third of the waters became wormwood, and many men died of the water, because it was made bitter" (Revelation 8:11). Wormwood symbolizes evil, the corruption of justice. *"O you who turn justice to wormwood, and cast down righteousness to the earth"* (Amos 5:7). The great Christian apologist C. S. Lewis (1898–1963) named his apprentice devil "Wormwood" in *The Screwtape Letters.* Wormwood the devil was being coached by a senior demon in methods of tempting and seducing a human and trying to secure his damnation.

"A third part of you shall die of pestilence and be consumed with famine in the midst of you; a third part of you shall fall by the sword round about you; and a third part I will scatter to all the winds and will unsheathe the sword after them" (Ezekiel 5:12) shows that the expression "one third" is common in prophetic language. Here a third of the earth was burnt up, and a third of the trees were burnt up, and a third of the sea became blood. Even though there is an obvious escalation of the damage in these plagues with respect to the earlier series, more escape intact than are destroyed. People are not affected here, which shows this is a warning that invites repentance. However, as it was with pharaoh in Egypt, the human heart may be hardened and slow to convert.

"Then I looked, and I heard an eagle crying with a loud voice, as it flew in midheaven, 'Woe, woe, woe to those who dwell on the earth, at the blasts of the other trumpets which the three angels are about to blow'" (Revelation 8:13). The stubbornness of humanity is why the four trumpets result in this preliminary vision of three woes: an eagle is soaring high in the skies so that all can see it. *"Wherever the body is, there the eagles will be gathered together"* (Matthew 24:28). The eagle announces a triple woe to those who refuse to fear God, repent and turn to Him. There are numerous references pointing to the time of judgment that will come (Revelation 3:10; 6:10; 8:13; 11:10; 13:8,14; 14:6–7; 17:8). Something even more dreadful is about to happen to humanity.

We do not of course desire the end of the world. Nevertheless, we do want this unjust world to end. We also want the world to be fundamentally changed; we want the beginning of the civilization of love, the arrival of a world of justice and peace, without violence, without hunger. We want all this, yet how can it happen without Christ's presence? Without Christ's presence there will never be a truly just and renewed world. And even if we do so in a different way, we too can and must also say, completely and profoundly, with great urgency and amid the circumstances of our time: "Come, Lord Jesus!"

(Pope Benedict XVI,
General Audience, November 12, 2008)

1. Use a dictionary or the *Catechism of the Catholic Church* to discuss eschatology.

CCC 1001
CCC 2771

2. What did Jesus say about the "End Times"?

Matthew 24:1–28
Mark 13:1–23
Luke 21:5–33

3. Will Jesus come again? And if so, how will He come?

Matthew 24:29–31
Mark 13:24–27
Luke 21:25–28
1 Corinthians 15:52
1 Thessalonians 4:14–16

* What does the Nicene Creed (Sunday liturgy) say about Jesus' return?

* What does the Apostles' Creed say about the Lord's return?

4. Describe the four horsemen. Zechariah 1:8–10, Revelation 6:1–8

White	
Red	
Black	
Pale	

5. Compare the following verses:

Ezekiel 5:12	
Hosea 13:14	
Matthew 24:21	
Mark 13:8	
Revelation 6:8	

* How could you prepare spiritually and practically for famine or tribulation?

6. Find a common thread in these verses.

Genesis 4:10
Psalm 79:1–5
Revelation 6:9–11

7. Describe the drama in Revelation 6:12–17.

8. What happens in the following verses?

Zechariah 6:4–5
Revelation 7:1

9. How many servants were sealed for God? Revelation 7:4–8

* What is the significance of their number?

** What would you say to someone who says that literally 144,000 will be saved?

10. Explain the importance of a being sealed for God.

Exodus 12:7–14
Ezekiel 9:4
2 Corinthians 1:21–22
Ephesians 1:11–14
Revelation 7:3–4

* Have you and your loved ones been sealed for God?

11. How and when were you sealed for God?

CCC 1294–1295
CCC 1296–1297

12. Describe the drama in Revelation 7:9–12.

13. Who is described in Revelation 7:13–14?

14. What can you learn from these verses?

Genesis 49:11
Revelation 7:14

* How will the martyrs be protected? Revelation 7:15

** Has there been a time in your life when you felt you had no one to shelter you?

15. Compare the following verses:

Psalm 121:6
Isaiah 49:10
Revelation 7:16

16. Find the hope in these verses:

Isaiah 25:8
Ezekiel 34:22–23
Revelation 7:17

17. Who can you find in these passages?

Tobit 12:15
Daniel 12:1–5
Psalm 141:2
Revelation 8:1–5

18. What common characteristic is found in the following verses?

Habakkuk 2:20
Zephaniah 1:7
Zechariah 2:13
Revelation 8:1

19. Identify a common occurrence in these verses:

Exodus 9:24–26		Revelation 8:7
Exodus 7:20–24		Revelation 8:9
Jeremiah 9:15		Revelation 8:11
Exodus 10:22		Revelation 8:12

20. Describe the angels, trumpets and woes in Revelation 8:6–13.

Chapter 16

Bitter but Sweet
Revelation 9–11

Then the voice which I had heard from heaven spoke to me again, saying,
"Go, take the scroll which is open in the hand of the angel
who is standing on the sea and on the land."
So I went to the angel and told him to give me the little scroll; and he said to me,
"Take it and eat; it will be bitter to your stomach,
but sweet as honey in your mouth."
Revelation 10:8–9

The fifth trumpet (Revelation 9:1–12)—The plague announced by this trumpet has its forerunner in the eighth plague of Egypt, when the east wind brought locusts over the whole land (Exodus 10:14). *"And the fifth angel blew his trumpet, and I saw a star fallen from heaven to earth, and he was given the key of the shaft of the bottomless pit … Then from the smoke came locusts on the earth, and they were given power like the power of scorpions"* (Revelation 9:1, 3). First, a mysterious star is seen falling from heaven, which is either an angel sent down by God to unlock the abyss (Revelation 1:20; 20:1) as a demonstration of the Lord's control over these plagues, or better, one of the fallen angels. Isaiah identifies one of them, Lucifer. *"How you are fallen from heaven, O Day Star, son of Dawn! How you are cut down to the ground, you who laid the nations low"* (Isaiah 14:12).

The abyss is the habitat where the demons live (Revelation 11:7; 17:8; 20:1–3). These locust-like creatures torture those who choose to belong to Satan (*Abaddon* in Hebrew, *Apollyon* in Greek) and his minions, causing bodily and spiritual pain for five months (Matthew 25:30; Luke 12:5; 14:9; 16:28–29). The details of their appearance include a monstrous composite of features that symbolize the gruesomeness and devilishness of the assault. *"Behold, I have given you authority to tread upon serpents and scorpions, and over all the power of the enemy; and nothing shall hurt you"* (Luke 10:19) proves how proverbial the venomous sting of the scorpion was in biblical times. The link between Abaddon, meaning destroyer, and Sheol, the grave, can be seen in: *"Sheol is naked before God, and Abaddon has no covering"* (Job 26:6). Also, *"Is your mercy declared in the grave, or your faithfulness in Abaddon?"* (Psalm 88:11).

The sixth trumpet (Revelation 9:13–19)—God has absolute control over these plagues. Another horrifying portrayal of a locust infestation is found in Joel 1–2. And, only when God speaks is the scourge unleashed. Four angels will act as generals of countless troops of cavalry (Revelation 7:1), stressing God's dominion over the vicissitudes of history. Some commentators have seen the feared Parthian invaders, whose border was the Euphrates, in these images. The surreal mingling of the visual qualities of the troops of cavalry, the horses and riders (Revelation 9:17–19) reminds us of Job's description of the sea-monster Leviathan:

> "His sneezings flash forth light,
>   and his eyes are like the eyelids of the dawn.
> Out of his mouth go flaming torches;
>   sparks of fire leap forth.
> Out of his nostrils comes forth smoke,
>   as from a boiling pot and burning rushes.
> His breath kindles coals,
>   and a flame comes forth from his mouth" (Job 41:18–21).

What is the purpose of all this devastation? God wants to bring about conversion from idolatry and the mindless depravity typical of the pagan world (see Isaiah 44:9–20; Psalm 115:4–8; Amos 4:6–11). Again, the fluidity and timelessness of apocalyptic imagery allows it to be applied to any period of world and Church history, including our own. Can you see mindless depravity today?

First interlude: the angel and the little scroll (Revelation 10:1–11)—First, look at the textual structure at this point. Recall Revelation 7 offered two visions: one hundred forty-four thousand sealed, and the multitude before the Lamb's throne, which signaled a break or interlude between the sixth and seventh seals. Here also are two interstitial visions—a little scroll, and two witnesses (Revelation 10–11), between the sixth and seventh trumpets. The title of this interlude could well be: "*Children, it is the last hour*" (1 John 2:18). Turning then to the vision about the little scroll, "*Then I saw another mighty angel coming down from heaven, wrapped in a cloud, with a rainbow over his head, and his face was like the sun, and his legs like pillars of fire. He had a little scroll open in his hand*" (Revelation 10:1–2), we recall that Ezekiel provided the Old Testament backdrop for this vision. "*I looked, behold, a hand was stretched out to me, and behold, a written scroll was in it; and he spread it before me; and it had writing on the front and on the back, and there were written on it words of lamentation and mourning and woe*" (Ezekiel 2:9–10).

This depiction of the mighty angel is very Christ-like to the point of a fusion, precisely like the Old Testament "*angel of the LORD*" (Exodus 3:2) who on his part is often totally merged into the divinity, highlighting the impact of his mission. Specifically, the "cloud" and "rainbow" imagery is explained with the help of familiar Old Testament passages. "*I set my bow in the cloud, and it shall be a sign of the covenant between me and the earth*" (Genesis 9:13). "*You are clothed with honor and majesty … who make the clouds your chariot, who ride on the wings of the wind*" (Psalm 104:1, 3). *I saw in the night visions, and behold, with the clouds*

150

of heaven there came one like a son of man" (Daniel 7:13). A "lion's roar" can be found in: *"The LORD will roar from on high"* (Jeremiah 25:30), *"They shall go after the LORD, he will roar like a lion"* (Hosea 11:10), and *"The LORD roars from Zion"* (Amos 1:2). The personified "thunder claps" represent the voice of God. *"The voice of the LORD is upon the waters; the God of glory thunders"* (Psalm 29:3). "Sun" and "pillars of fire" echo Old Testament passages that speak of God's utter unapproachability and radiant majesty.

Arguably, the little scroll open in the angel's hand (Revelation 10:2) stands for the essence of the Good News, unlike the previous scroll with its seven seals (Revelation 5:1), which envisioned primarily the destiny of the Church in world history. The angel's mission is vast, without frontiers, indicated by one foot on sea and another on the land, and the message is clear, shown by the open scroll. Paradoxically, the universal judgment is still far off, whereas the imminence of the end is stated clearly. Similar to Daniel 12:2–9, John on Patmos is ordered to seal up the revelation he has received. Here the truth is revealed that Christ has already triumphed in His Death and Resurrection, but Judgment is completed only at the end of history when Jesus will return in glory (Revelation 11:13ff).

When the seventh trumpet is sounded, there shall be no more delay. The "mystery of God" will be accomplished—the establishment of the kingdom of God on earth through the Church. For Saint Paul the mystery is the inclusion of the Gentiles in that Church and the eventual conversion of Israel (Romans 11:25; 16:25–26; 1 Corinthians 2:11; Ephesians 1:9ff; 3:3; Colossians 1:26ff; 2:2; 4:3; 2 Thessalonians 2:6). Eating the word of God and perceiving its sweetness and bitterness is a form of prophetic initiation or investiture that was also present in Ezekiel 3:1–3. The Seer is to proclaim a word that he has first made his own. Christ's victory causes the message to be sweet, but that necessary tribulation that accompanies the pilgrimage of Jesus' Gospel through the ages is bitter. *"Every tribe and people and tongue and nation"* (Revelation 13:7; 14:6; 17:15; Jeremiah 1:5–10) are the audience for that transforming Word. This marvelously illustrates that the Apocalypse is essentially a religious interpretation of history, indeed, the *Theology of History*.

Second interlude: the two witnesses (Revelation 11:1–14)—The Apostle on Patmos is given a tool to take measurements of the temple, altar and worshippers. The measuring rod or measuring line also appears in Old Testament passages in Ezekiel 40:1–43:17, Zechariah 2:1–5, and 2 Samuel 8:2b. Preservation seems to be the point of this prophetic gesture. The true adorers of God, deriving from Israel, will enjoy divine protection always. The court outside the temple may signify Judaism and the synagogue separated from the Church. Their fate is alluded to in the words *"nations will trample over the holy city"* (Revelation 11:2). The refusal of the Jews as a nation to believe in Christ caused their temporary exclusion (Romans 11:25). Some consider this image to relate solely to the Church. The outer court points to persecutions, and the inner sanctuary depicts her hidden interior life before God.

Other symbols to be deciphered are the *"forty-two months"* and the *"one thousand two hundred and sixty days"* (forty-two months = three and a half years), or *"a time, and times, and half a time"* (Revelation 11:2–3; 12:14), foreshadowed already in Daniel 7:25; 9:27, and 12:7. Drought of approximately that length of time occurs earlier in the Bible (1 Kings 17) and is recalled in the New Testament as well (Luke 4:25). This numerical symbol stresses the times of persecution and hardship of a limited duration in the history of the Church.

"And I will grant my two witnesses power to prophesy for one thousand two hundred and sixty days, clothed in sackcloth" (Revelation 11:3). Many interpretations have been proposed for the two witnesses: Moses and Elijah, Enoch and Elijah, Peter and Paul, or the hearts of Jesus and Mary. The Prophet Zechariah has previously introduced two olive trees representing Joshua and Zerubbabel, the supreme representatives of the priesthood and royalty (Zechariah 4:11–14). Keep in mind that the olive tree serves as a sign of testimony to God. *"And if any one would harm them, fire pours from their mouth and consumes their foes"* (Revelation 11:5) clearly reminds of *"behold, I am making my words in your mouth a fire, and this people wood, and the fire shall devour them"* (Jeremiah 5:14). In ultimate analysis, it is likely that the two witnesses together represent the Church in her timeless preaching of the Gospel of Christ. In Jesus' teaching, the Law of old, epitomized by Moses, and the Prophets, typified by Elijah, comes to full fruition. *"So whatever you wish that men would do to you, do so to them; for this is the law and the prophets"* (Matthew 7:12).

"And when they have finished their testimony, the beast that ascends from the bottomless pit will make war upon them" (Revelation 11:7). The beast figuratively represents all hostility against God's plans. Evil emerges in the reality of a *"great city, called Sodom and Egypt"* (Revelation 11:8). This city is later identified as Babylon (Revelation 14:8; 16:19; 17:5; 18:2, 10) indicating the Roman Empire at that time, and all worldly power opposed to God down through the centuries. Babylon and Jerusalem *"where their Lord was crucified"* (Revelation 11:8) are code names for the Roman Empire. They all synthesize the martyrdom of the Church at the hand of her enemies throughout history. The resurrection of those witnesses (martyrs) is prefigured in Ezekiel's valley of dry bones, which receives the breath of new life. Israel's captivity prefigures the Church. Like Jesus, who ascended to His Father in Heaven (Acts 1:9), the witnesses are transported into heaven by a cloud in acceptance of their sacrificial ministry. *"Then they heard a loud voice from heaven saying to them, 'Come up here!' And in the sight of their foes they went up to heaven in a cloud"* (Revelation 11:12). Saint John seems to anticipate the grand finale of salvation history at this point. Does the repentance of the rest hint at the final acceptance of Christ by the Jewish people (Romans 11:25–27)? The earthquake and seventh trumpet mark the dramatic conclusion of the first part of Revelation.

The seventh trumpet (Revelation 11:15–19)—We could label this section, Revelation 11:15–20:15, the decisive struggle between God and Satan for Lordship of the world. Obviously, the dualism here is relative, not absolute, because of the definitive victory already won by the Lamb. Thus, the forces of evil are at all times subject to Christ's paramount authority. Evil is permitted to act out in order to test everyone's free will. *"The kingdom of the world has become the kingdom of our Lord and of his Christ, and he shall reign for ever and ever"* (Revelation 11:15) zooms the lens in on heaven again as the seventh trumpet sounds, signaling Jesus' triumph. This verse should be familiar to everyone, since it reaches climatic proportions in the singing of George Frideric Handel's magnificent (1741) *Messiah*.

Now the time comes to reward *"your servants, the prophets and saints, and those who fear your name, both small and great"* (Revelation 11:18), that is, the just of both Testaments, who have been waiting for redemption from God. *"And all these, though well attested by their faith, did not receive what was promised, since God had foreseen something better for us, that apart from us they should not be made perfect"* (Hebrews 11:39–40). Eloquently, the Seer catches a glimpse of the Ark of the Covenant, *"Then God's temple in heaven was opened, and the ark of his covenant was seen within his temple"* (Revelation 11:19a). Previously, Jeremiah had been instructed by God to conceal it in a cavern on Mount Nebo. *"Jeremiah came and found a cave, and he brought there the tent and the ark and the altar of incense, and he sealed up the entrance … until God gathers his people together again and shows his mercy"* (2 Maccabees 2:5–7).

"Then God's temple in heaven was opened, and the ark of his covenant was seen within his temple; and there were flashes of lightning, loud noises, peals of thunder, an earthquake, and heavy hail" (Revelation 11:19). This eye-catching cosmic turbulence simply underscores divine power and presence. Earlier, when God spoke to Moses on Mount Sinai there was smoke and fire, thunder and lightning, the whole mountain quaked and *"God answered him in thunder"* (Exodus 19:16–19). So, these extraordinary manifestations of nature can accompany the presence of the glorious God revealing his power to humanity.

But when they see how those who have sinned and who have denied Jesus by their words or by their deeds are punished with terrible torture in unquenchable fire, the just, who have done good, and who have endured tortures and have hated the luxuries of life, will give glory to their God, saying, "There shall be hope for him that has served God with all his heart."

(Saint Clement of Rome, [† 99 AD], *Second Letter to the Corinthians*, 17,7)

1. Identify the star fallen from heaven.

Isaiah 14:12–15
Revelation 9:1

2. Find some similarities in the following places:

Genesis 19:28
Revelation 9:2

3. What is the significance of a seal?

Revelation 9:4
CCC 1296

* How and when have you been sealed for Christ?

4. Describe the tormenters.

Joel 2:4–6
Revelation 9:3–10

5. Identify the being in Revelation 9:11.

* How can you defend your self against him? 1 Peter 5:6–10, James 4:7

6. Describe the drama in Revelation 9:12–19.

7. How did the rest of mankind respond to the devastation? Revelation 9:20

* What would you do if you knew that your time on earth was coming to an end?

8. Identify a common thread in the following verses.

Jeremiah 25:30
Amos 3:8
Revelation 10:3

9. What can you learn from these passages?

Deuteronomy 32:40
Daniel 12:7
Revelation 10:5

10. What similar instruction is given to these prophets?

Ezekiel 2:8–9
Ezekiel 3:1–3
Revelation 10:9

11. Explain the commission given to these two servants of God.

Jeremiah 1:4–10
Revelation 10:11

* Identify a prophet of God in our times and explain.

** Did you ever feel like God was asking you to speak to someone? Did you obey?

12. Describe the activity in the following passages:

Ezekiel 42:15–19
Revelation 11:1
Revelation 21:15

13. What will happen in these passages?

Zechariah 12:3
Isaiah 63:18
Luke 21:24
Revelation 11:2

14. What is the significance of the lampstands and olive trees?

Zechariah 4:2–14
Revelation 11:4–8

* How can you, as a Christian, be like a lampstand or a witness?

15. What did the beast do to the witnesses? Revelation 11:7–8

16. How do the people react to martyrdom? Revelation 11:9–10

17. What does God do? Revelation 11:11–12

18. Explain something about the center of history or kingdoms.

Psalm 22:28–29
Daniel 7:14, 27
Revelation 11:15
CCC 450

19. What kind of prayer do the twenty-four elders pray? Revelation 11:17–18

20. What happens in Revelation 11:19?

* What kind of prayer would you pray if you saw the heavens opened?

Chapter 17

The Woman
Revelation 12

And a great portent appeared in heaven,
a woman clothed with the sun,
with the moon under her feet, and on her head a crown of twelve stars;
she was with child and she cried out in her pangs of birth,
in anguish for delivery.
Revelation 12:1–2

The Woman and the Dragon (Revelation 12:1–18)—Let us first take a look at the subdivision of this crucial chapter:
1) Revelation 12:1–4a = two symbolic persons, the woman and the dragon;
2) Revelation 12:4b–12 = the Messiah;
3) Revelation 12:13–18 = persecution of the woman's offspring.

Our sacred writer masterfully merges biblical symbols and texts. A great sign is contrasted with the simple sign of the dragon, which reveals a profound truth. *"Who is this that looks forth like the dawn, fair as the moon, bright as the sun, terrible as an army with banners?"* (Song of Songs 6:10) prefigures the Woman of Revelation. *"Arise, shine; for your light has come, and the glory of the LORD has risen upon you. For behold, darkness shall cover the earth, and thick darkness the peoples; but the LORD will arise upon you, and his glory will be seen upon you. And nations shall walk by your light, and kings in the brightness of your rising"* (Isaiah 60:1–3), prefigures the dawning of the Church. Sun and moon recall the two great lights of creation (Genesis 1:14–19). Joseph's dream of the sun, moon, and eleven stars bowing down to him, who will become the twelve tribes of Israel (Genesis 37:9) forms the prophetic background for the twelve stars.

"Like a woman with child, who writhes and cries out in her pangs, when she is near her time, so were we because of you, O LORD (Isaiah 26:17), and *"For as soon as Zion was in labor she brought forth her sons. Shall I bring to the birth and not cause to bring forth?"* (Isaiah 66:8–9) explain the cries amid the pangs of childbirth. *"Writhe and groan, O daughter of Zion, like a woman with labor pains; for now you shall go forth from the city and dwell in the open country; you shall go to Babylon. There you shall be rescued, there the LORD will redeem you from the hand of your enemies"* (Micah 4:10) prefigures the need for God to save humanity from sin, and draws attention to the coming of the messianic era. *"But when the time had fully come, God sent forth his Son, born of woman, born under the law, so that we might receive adoption as sons"* (Galatians 4:4). This mysterious Woman is bursting on the scene with the attributes of the ideal spiritual Zion, the New Jerusalem. *"But the Jerusalem above is free, and she is our mother"* (Galatians 4:26). She embodies the covenanted people of God, Israel

159

and the Church, and Mary, who has given birth to the Messiah surrounded by anguish and suffering. Jesus foretold this in His teachings. *"For nation will rise against nation, and kingdom against kingdom; there will be earthquakes in various places, there will be famines; this is but the beginning of the sufferings"* (Mark 13:8).

"And another sign appeared in heaven; behold, a great red dragon, with seven heads and ten horns, and seven diadems upon his heads. His tail swept down a third of the stars of heaven, and cast them to the earth" (Revelation 12:3–4a) reveals the face of evil under the figure of a great red dragon, the ancient Leviathan, the twisting monster of the deep. The Prophet Isaiah foretells that God will slay the evil dragon. *"In that day the LORD with his hard and great and strong sword will punish Leviathan the fleeing serpent, Leviathan the twisting serpent, and he will slay the dragon that is in the sea"* (Isaiah 27:1). Daniel also had a vision of this creature with horns upon its head (Daniel 7:7). Wearing the seven diadems on his head is a symbol of exceptional power. In his fury he sweeps down a third of the stars from heaven, hinting at the primordial fall of the angels.

"You shall break them with a rod of iron, and dash them in pieces like a potter's vessel" (Psalm 2:9) finds its most exhaustive exposition in predicting that the Messiah will rule the nations with an iron rod. *"She brought forth a male child, one who is to rule all the nations with a rod of iron, but her child was caught up to God and to his throne* (Revelation 12:5–12). This passage includes Christ's birth, Resurrection and Ascension. The wilderness is symbolic of the pilgrimage of the Church through time, nourished by God's providence.

Phased in a previous time is the image of the primeval strife and schism of the angels. *"Now war arose in heaven, Michael and his angels fighting against the dragon; and the dragon and his angels fought, but they were defeated and there was no longer any place for them in heaven. And the great dragon was thrown down, that ancient serpent, who is called the Devil and Satan, the deceiver of the whole world—he was thrown down to the earth, and his angels were thrown down with him"* (Revelation 12:7–9). This shows a dazzling superimposition of images beyond the barriers of space and time. Saint Michael's triumph over demonic rivals mirrors the victory of the Woman, the Virgin Mary, the New Eve. *"I will put enmity between you and the woman, and between your seed and her seed; he shall bruise your head, and you shall bruise his heel"* (Genesis 3:15).

The Blessed Mother becomes our Mother at the foot of the Cross, when Jesus says to the disciple, *"Behold, your mother!"* (John 19:27). As a consequence we hear the exultant hymn, *"Now the salvation and the power and the kingdom of our God and the authority of his Christ have come, for the accuser of our brethren has been thrown down, who accuses them day and night before our God. And they have conquered him by the blood of the Lamb and by the word of their testimony, for they loved not their lives even unto death. Rejoice then, O heaven and you that dwell therein! But woe to you, O earth and sea, for the devil has come down to you in great wrath, because he knows that his time is short"* (Revelation 12:10–12). This reaffirms that the devil has been vanquished by the blood of the Lamb.

> Mary the Virgin is found to be obedient, saying: *Behold, O Lord, your handmaid; be it done to me according to your word*" (Luke 1:38). Eve, however, was disobedient ... having become disobedient, was made the cause of death for herself and for the whole human race; so also Mary, betrothed to a man but nevertheless still a virgin, being obedient, was made the cause of salvation for herself and for the whole human race ... Thus, the knot of Eve's disobedience was loosed by the obedience of Mary. What the virgin Eve had bound in unbelief, the Virgin Mary loosed through faith.
>
> (Saint Irenaeus, [140–202 AD], *Against Heresies*, 3, 22, 4)

Christ Jesus is the Victor. *"For behold, the LORD will come in fire, and his chariots like the stormwind, to render his anger in fury, and his rebuke with flames of fire. For by fire will the LORD execute judgment, and by his sword, upon all flesh; and those slain by the LORD shall be many"* (Isaiah 66:15–16).

With his wrath redoubled the dragon makes war against the Woman's offspring. His rage is intense because his time is almost up. *"But the woman was given the two wings of the great eagle that she might fly from the serpent into the wilderness, to the place where she is to be nourished for a time, and times, and half a time"* (Revelation 12:14). To flee into the desert signifies God's care for His Church until Christ's return. *"I bore you on eagles' wings and brought you to myself"* (Exodus 19:4) recalls God's protection of His people in Egypt. *"They who wait for the LORD shall renew their strength, they shall mount up with wings like eagles, they shall run and not be weary, they shall walk and not faint"* (Isaiah 40:31) provides hope for people in the midst of trials and suffering.

The desert is a biblical image for finding refuge. The desert is the place for God's first love toward and espousal with His people. The dragon attempts to transform that wilderness into a pseudo-paradise by a sinister river issuing from his mouth, trying to delude the Church regarding her redemptive mission in this world. Yet, the devil's attack is thwarted by the earth, which symbolically swallows that deceptively distracting stream, shielding the woman and all her progeny from any fatal harm. Satan is faced with the decisive conflict and becomes angry, now that the judgment of this world has come through the conquest of Calvary. *"Now is the judgment of this world, now shall the ruler of this world be cast out; and I, when I am lifted up from the earth, will draw all men to myself"* (John 12:31–32).

It is perfectly legitimate to see in this breath-taking whirlwind of imagery a nutshell of the entire history of salvation. Mary the Mother is a type of the Church, stealthily besieged by the powers of darkness. Nevertheless, she travels and rests serene, knowing that her Lord is the Alpha and Omega, the Victor. A selection of opinions may be helpful to further grasp the depth of this text. Saint Hippolytus of Rome († 235 AD) said that the Woman signals the Church clothed with the divine Logos and surrounded by the sheen of the twelve apostles. She never ceases to give birth to the Word even as she overcomes any persecution by the unbelievers of this world. Saint Methodius of Olympia († 312 AD) said that through this Woman, Christ is born spiritually in the hearts of the faithful. Among those who assert that the Woman mystically personifies the Church are Saint Victorinus of Pettau († 304 AD), Saint Augustine of Hippo (354–430 AD), Saint Quodvultdeus of Carthage († 450), Saint Gregory the Great (540–604 AD), Saint Bonaventure (1221–1274 AD), and Saint Pius X (1835–1914 AD). Therefore, the Marian (individual) and ecclesiological (collective) interpretations are by no means mutually exclusive. The Catholic interpretation on Sacred Scripture embraces both symbolic meanings of the Woman in Revelation 12. Individually, the Blessed Virgin Mary is our Mother. Collectively, Holy Mother Church is our mother, as well.

Hymn on Blessed Mary

Awake, my harp, your songs
    In praise of the Virgin Mary!
Lift up your voice and sing
    the wonderful history
Of the Virgin, the daughter of David,
    who gave birth to the Life of the World.

Who loves you is amazed;
    and who cannot understand is silent and confused,
Because he cannot probe the Mother
    who gave birth in her virginity.
If it is too great to be clarified with words the disputants
    ought not on that account cross swords with your Son.

In the womb of Mary the Infant was formed,
    who from eternity is equal to the Father.
He imparted to us His greatness,
    and took on our infirmity.
He became mortal like us and joined his life to ours,
    so that we might die no more.

The Virgin became a Mother
    while preserving her virginity.
And though still a Virgin she carried a Child in her womb;
    And the handmaid and work of His Wisdom
became the Mother of God.

(Saint Ephraim [306–373 AD],
Hymns of the Nativity, 1. 1, 2, 12, 20)

Two Women of Revelation

Woman Clothed with the Sun	Whore of Babylon
Revelation 12:1–6	Revelation 17
A woman clothed with the sun, with the moon under her feet, and on her head a crown of twelve stars Revelation 12:1	A great harlot… sitting on a scarlet beast full of blasphemous names Revelation 17:1, 30
The dragon sought to devour her child when she brought it forth Revelation 12:4	The woman was clothed in purple and scarlet, gold and jewels… holding a cup full of abominations and the impurities of her fornication Revelation 17:4
She brought forth a male child, who will rule the nations with a rod of iron Revelation 12:5	The woman [was] drunk with the blood of the saints and the blood of the martyrs of Jesus. Revelation 17:6
Her child was caught up to God and to his throne Revelation 12:5b	The beast will hate the harlot; they will make her desolate and naked, and devour her flesh and burn her up with fire. Revelation 17:16
The woman fled into the wilderness, where she has a place prepared by God Revelation 12:6	Seven hills on which the woman sits Revelation 17:9
	The woman is the great city which has dominion over the kings of the earth Revelation 17:18

1. Identify those who take part in the heavenly service praising God. CCC 1138

2. Who appears in Revelation 12:1?

3. Research and describe at least one Marian apparition in which Our Lady appeared with a crown of twelve stars over her head.

4. What can you learn from comparing these verses?

Micah 4:10	
Revelation 12:2	

5. Discuss several ways in which the woman in Revelation 12 may be interpreted.

* Find one Marian apparition in which the serpent is under Mary's feet.

6. Identify phrases, that compare Mary to the Ark of the Covenant.

2 Samuel 6:18	Luke 1:42
2 Samuel 6:9	Luke 1:43
2 Samuel 6:16	Luke 1:44
2 Samuel 6:11	Luke 1:56

7. Who shows up in these passages?

Daniel 7:7–25
Revelation 12:3–4

8. What did the dragon try to do? Revelation 12:4

9. Who is the woman pursued by the dragon? CCC 2853

10. Who is described in these passages?

Isaiah 66:7–9	
Luke 2:7	
Revelation 12:5	

11. Describe the drama in Revelation 12:7–9.

12. Identify three names of the evil one found in Revelation 12:9.

13. What can you learn about the serpent, the evil one?

Genesis 3:1, 14–15	
Zechariah 3:1–2	
CCC 391	
CCC 2852	

14. How can you fight the devil? James 4:7–10; 1 Peter 5:8–10

15. What does Saint John hear in heaven?

Isaiah 44:23–26
Isaiah 49:13–16
Revelation 12:10–12

16. Describe the drama in Revelation 12:13–16.

17. Who are the offspring of the woman? Revelation 12:17

18. Explain Mary's spiritual motherhood. CCC 501

19. How is Holy Mother Church your mother? CCC 757

20. Share your favorite Marian prayer and Marian hymn with your group.

* How could you come to have a closer relationship with our Blessed Mother?

Chapter 18

Beast and Lamb
Revelation 13–14

Then I looked, and lo, on Mount Zion stood the Lamb,
and with him a hundred and forty-four thousand
who had his name
and his Father's name
written on their foreheads.
Revelation 14:1

The beast from the sea (Revelation 13:1–10)—"*And I saw a beast rising out of the sea, with ten horns and seven heads, with ten diadems upon its horns and a blasphemous name upon its heads*" (Revelation 13:1). Similar to the dragon of the preceding chapter (Revelation 12:3), who has only seven diadems, this beast emerging from the sea has ten diadems pointing to an absolute concentration of power. This image forges into one the four beasts of Daniel 7, and embodies worldly kingdoms like Babylon and Persia. This satanic power is bent on making an absolute claim on man. For John's audience, the beast was the Roman Empire of their time. Prudence forces the Seer to employ coded language here. We will explain the symbolism of heads, horns and crowns in Revelation 17:9–14. This beast from the sea is the continuation of the dragon's presence in history. "*One of its heads seemed to have a mortal wound, but its mortal wound was healed*" (Revelation 13:3), provides perverse parody as it pretends to be mortally wounded like the Lamb of God, who actually did die for the sins of the world.

As this beast succeeds in its travesty of the truth and thus deceives and confuses the inhabitants of the earth, they wind up worshipping it, mesmerized by its pomp and power. Their words of flattery, "*Who is like the beast, and who can fight against it?*" (Revelation 13: 4b), mimic the awe of triumph and wonder that the people of God expressed after seeing the power of God after the Exodus. "*Who is like you, O LORD, among the gods? Who is like you, majestic in holiness, terrible in glorious deeds, doing wonders*" (Exodus 15:11). Elihu asks a probing question, "*Who teaches us more than the beasts of the earth, and makes us wiser than the birds of the air*" (Job 35:11). Saint Paul warns believers to keep guard against the deceptions of evil. "*Let no one deceive you in any way, for that day will not come, unless the rebellion comes first, and the man of lawlessness is revealed, the son of perdition, who opposes and exalts himself against every so-called god or object of worship, so that he takes his seat in the temple of God, proclaiming himself to be God*" (2 Thessalonians 2:3–4).

The blaspheming beast, "*it opened its mouth to utter blasphemies against God, blaspheming his name and his dwelling, that is, those who dwell in heaven*" (Revelation 13:6) resembles the fourth monster of Daniel 7:8 with its small horn that divulged great things. Likewise, *"He shall speak words against the Most High, and shall wear out the saints of the Most High, and shall think to change the times and the law; and they shall be given into his hand for a time, two times, and half a time"* (Daniel 7:25) is pivotal to understand the actions of the beast, who utters words against the Almighty and oppresses the saints for a limited amount of time. *"Also it was allowed to make war on the saints and to conquer them"* (Revelation 13:7). This verse reassures the reader that God, who is the ultimate Sovereign of creation and history, permits or allows all of this turmoil only for a time. Thankfully, there are a number of people who do not fall for the beast: those whose names are recorded in the book of the Lamb. Christians are not called to rebel against this evil reality nor must they adore it. Rather, they are called to endure and persevere in their dedication to the one true God.

The beast from the land (Revelation 13:11–18)—The beast from the land appears deceptively similar to the Lamb. This beast is really imbued with the spirit of the dragon. It acts in the name of the first beast and serves as its mouthpiece, speaking blasphemy and false prophecy *"it spoke like a dragon"* (Revelation 13:11b). The reader is alerted to discern true from false prophecy (Revelation 16:13; 19:20; 20:10). Jesus warned: *"For false Christs and false prophets will arise and show great signs and wonders, so as to lead astray, if possible, even the elect"* (Matthew 24:24). The beast is allowed to work signs and wonders, *"It works great signs, even making fire come down from heaven to earth in the sight of men"* (Revelation 13:13). But the believer has been alerted and is prepared to discern the signs that come from God from the signs and wonders of the evil one. *"The coming of the lawless one by the activity of Satan will be with all power and with pretended signs and wonders, and with all wicked deception for those who are to perish, because they refused to love the truth and so be saved"* (2 Thessalonians 2:9–10).

The fire coming down from heaven may be a subtle reference to the Old Testament Prophet Elijah, who called down fire from heaven to expose the false prophets of Baal (1 Kings 18:38). Emperor cult worship was demanded by Rome in the first century as a bond of cosmopolitan unity, and Christians were forced to offer libations of wine and water before the statue of the emperor. Thus, the second beast parodies the Holy Spirit who alone has spoken through the prophets. *"Also it causes all, both small and great, both rich and poor, both free and slave, to be marked on the right hand or forehead"* (Revelation 13:16). This mark is reminiscent of a sort of tattoo or brand that was used in antiquity to distinguish slaves and soldiers from ordinary citizens. This mark again apes the seal of the Lord impressed on those who enjoy His protection and salvation. *"Do not harm the earth or the sea or the trees, till we have sealed the servants of our God upon their foreheads"* (Revelation 7:3). As Christians we are sealed with an indelible sacramental mark in Baptism, Confirmation, and Holy Orders.

"This calls for wisdom: let him who has understanding reckon the number of the beast, for it is a human number, its number is six hundred and sixty-six" (Revelation 13:18) gives us a flair of wisdom literature. Here, the reader is required to become even more actively involved in solving the mystery of the number of the beast. If seven is a symbol

of perfection, then 666 points to complete imperfection. All other explanations and applications of this numerical value to concrete personalities in history fall short. One is always well advised to keep the images of the apocalyptic genre as timeless as possible. The opposite of good is evil. The opposite of a true prophet is a false prophet. The opposite of Christ is called the Antichrist. Antichrist is simply a false prophet who exalts himself rather than God. Beasts, dragons, false prophets, and antichrists all belong to the dominion of evil. The task of the believer is to keep one's eyes fixed on God, the Supreme Good.

The Lamb on Mount Zion (Revelation 14:1–5)—*"Then I looked, and behold, on Mount Zion stood the Lamb, and with him a hundred and forty-four thousand who had his name and his Father's name written on their foreheads"*(Revelation 14:1). Prophetically speaking, Zion is the traditional site where Israel's remnant will congregate as the core of the messianic Kingdom. *"And it shall come to pass that all who call upon the name of the LORD shall be delivered; for in Mount Zion and in Jerusalem there shall be those who escape, as the LORD has said, and among the survivors shall be those whom the LORD calls"* (Joel 2:32; see also 2 Kings 19:30ff). Mount Zion is the epitome of Israel's refuge and hope, and it is there that the visionary of Patmos beholds the one hundred forty-four thousand. They have reached their goal at last and intone the "new song" of their beatific vision. How are we to understand the defilement mentioned in *"It is these who have not defiled themselves with women, for they are chaste"* (Revelation14:4)? This certainly does not refer to a particular state of life in the Church, nor exclusively to the unmarried. It has to be read in the light of the traditional prophetic comparison between idolatry and adultery, spoken of by Jeremiah, Ezekiel, and Hosea.

Those who have not succumbed to false worship are compared to faithful spouses. Faithful Christians are often described in bridal metaphors. *"Let us rejoice and exult and give him the glory, for the marriage of the Lamb has come, and his Bride has made herself ready; it was granted her to be clothed with fine linen, bright and pure—for the fine linen is the righteous deeds of the saints"* (Revelation 19:7–8). Saint Paul uses similar bridal imagery, *"I feel a divine jealousy for you, for I betrothed you to Christ to present you as a pure bride to her one husband"* (2 Corinthians 11:2). The Prophet Jeremiah provides a clue to understanding the passage: *"these who follow the Lamb wherever he goes; these have been redeemed from mankind as first fruits for God and the Lamb"* (Revelation 14:4b). Jeremiah says: *"Israel was holy to the LORD, the first fruits of his harvest"* (Jeremiah 2:3).

Proclamation of the hour of judgment (Revelation 14:6–13)—A *first* angel is sent out with a message of repentance, *"Fear God and give him glory, for the hour of his judgment has come"* (Revelation 14:6). The angel gives a proclamation of the gospel and an invitation to repentance, much as a human evangelist would do. Saint Peter exhorts, *"Repent therefore, and turn again, that your sins may be blotted out"* (Acts 3:19). Saint Paul reports, *"you turned to God from idols, to serve a living and true God, and to wait for his Son from heaven, whom he raised from the dead, Jesus who delivers us from the wrath to come"* (1 Thessalonians 1:9–10). A *second* angel surprises us with the proclamation of Babylon's fall: *"Fallen, fallen is Babylon the great, she who made all nations drink the wine of her impure passion"* (Revelation 14:8). Isaiah received an oracle, which foretold this event. *"Fallen, fallen is Babylon; and all the images of her gods he has shattered to the ground"* (Isaiah 21:9). Babylon epitomizes any moral degradation and religious depletion. Babylon's "impure passion" is precisely the idolatry (= immorality) that the faithful multitude in Revelation 14:4 had avoided.

But then there emerges a *third* angel, with a frightening announcement regarding the punishment of those who have given in to the beast. *"If any one worships the beast and its image, and receives a mark on his forehead or on his hand, he also shall drink the wine of God's wrath, poured unmixed into the cup of his anger, and he shall be tormented with fire and brimstone in the presence of the holy angels and in the presence of the Lamb. And the smoke of their torment goes up for ever and ever; and they have no rest, day or night, these worshipers of the beast and its image, and whoever receives the mark of its name"* (Revelation 14:9–12). Their fate is truly dreadful, evoking images of the annihilation of Sodom and Gomorrah: *"Then the LORD rained on Sodom and Gomorrah brimstone and fire from the LORD out of heaven"* (Genesis 19:24).

Isaiah the Prophet foretells the wrath of the Lord. *"Rouse yourself, rouse yourself, stand up, O Jerusalem, you who have drunk at the hand of the LORD the cup of his wrath, who have drunk to the dregs the bowl of staggering"* (Isaiah 51:17). Jeremiah also forewarns of the Lord's wrath: *"Take from my hand this cup of the wine of wrath, and make all the nations to whom I send you drink it. They shall drink and stagger and be crazed because of the sword which I am sending among them"* (Jeremiah 25:15ff). The cup of God's wrath stands for divine chastisement, the judgment of God upon the wicked. What is most shocking about the lot of those evildoers is that their torment goes on forever and ever. Isaiah foretold this eternal punishment: *"And they shall go forth and look on the dead bodies of the men that have rebelled against me; for their worm shall not die, their fire shall not be quenched, and they shall be an abhorrence to all flesh"* (Isaiah 66:24). But the thrust of the message is to instill courage and patience in the hearers, the faithful believers. *"Here is a call for the endurance of the saints, those who keep the commandments of God and the faith of Jesus"* (Revelation 14:12). Finally, what makes this passage complete is the book's second beatitude, addressed to all those who will die in the Lord, most especially those who will shed their blood in testimony for Him. *"Blessed are the dead who from now on died in the Lord"* (Revelation 14:13) praises the early Christian martyrs and those of all ages.

Reaping the earth's harvest (Revelation 14:14–20)—John now discloses another vision, presenting God's judgment as the reaping of a harvest or the treading of the wine press, metaphors that stem from Isaiah 17:5; 27:12; 63:3–6; Jeremiah 25:30; and Joel 3:13. John the Baptist introduces Jesus as the One who *"will baptize you with the Holy Spirit and with fire. His winnowing fork is in his hand, and he will clear his threshing floor and gather his wheat into the granary, but the chaff he will burn with unquenchable fire"* (Matthew 3:12). The Son of Man appears again here in Revelation 14:14, fulfilling the prophecy of Daniel 7:13ff, positioned between two formations of three angels each.

"Then I looked, and behold, a white cloud, and seated on the cloud one like a son of man, with a golden crown on his head, and a sharp sickle in his hand" (Revelation 14:14). His golden crown reveals Him as King, the cloud reveals Him as God, and the sickle reveals Him as Judge. Apocalyptic literature has a predilection for dramatization, which is the reason why the temple angel calls out to Him inviting Him to initiate the harvest. But what remains unequivocally clear is that God alone determines the hour. Christ's Parousia, His Second Coming, is more fully pictured in Revelation 19:11–21.

Other angels ready themselves to assist the divine Master of the harvest. In hindsight a connection is established with the souls of the martyrs crying out from the altar for vengeance (6:10). The symbol of the winepress trodden outside the city of Jerusalem evokes a Jewish belief according to which the Last Judgment over Israel's enemies will be held in the nearby valley of Jehoshaphat. *"I will gather all the nations and bring them down to the valley of Jehoshaphat, and I will enter into judgment with them there, on account of my people and my heritage Israel"* (Joel 3:2). As a result of the vintage, blood flows abundantly to cover the whole world, symbolized by the one thousand six hundred stadia. Four times four times one hundred equals one thousand six hundred (4 x 4 x 100 = 1600) represents geographic universality (the four compass points). This is a way of telling the reader that the Judgment has acquired cosmic proportions. It is also reasonable that the metaphor of the harvest implies the gathering of the elect, whereas the image of the vintage intends to represent the chastisement of the wicked.

> We invoke You, the Increate, through Your Only-begotten in the Holy Spirit. Be merciful to this people ... We beseech You also on behalf of all the departed, of whom also this is the commemoration ... Sanctify these souls, for You know them all; sanctify all who have fallen asleep in the Lord and count them all among the ranks of Your saints and give them a place and abode in Your kingdom.
>
> (Bishop Serapion of Thmuis, Egypt,
> *The Sacramentary of Serapion* [350 AD], 13.1)

1. Explain idolatry. CCC 2113

2. Describe some common characteristics of the beasts in Daniel and Revelation.

Daniel 7:4	Revelation 13:2 *"mouth like a*
Daniel 7:5	Revelation 13:2 *"feet like a*
Daniel 7:6	Revelation 13:2 *"like a*
Daniel 7:7 *"it had _____ horns"*	Revelation 13:1 *"with ____ horns"*

3. Identify the genuine "Suffering Servant" and the fraud, who appears to suffer.

Isaiah 53:5
Revelation 13:3

4. Describe authentic worship and demonic worship.

Matthew 2:10–11
Luke 4:8
Revelation 5:9
Revelation 13:4

5. Explain the relationship between the dragon and the beast. Revelation 13:4–6

6. What must take place for the Church to enter into glory?

Revelation 13:8–10
CCC 677

7. What two virtues must the saints have? Revelation 13:10b

* Discuss some practical ways in which you could grow in these virtues.

8. What warning of God is disobeyed here?

Deuteronomy 13:1–5
Revelation 13:11–15

* How can a believer resist following the crowd into evil?

9. The Hebrews letters of Caesar Nero's name equal 666. What can you learn about Nero's persecution of the Church that would suggest a good fit here? Revelation 13:18

10. What will be experienced in the heavenly liturgy?

Revelation 14:1–3
CCC 1137

* What is the most heavenly liturgy you have experienced?

11. Explain the significance of a name and a mark.

Ezekiel 9:4
Revelation 14:1
CCC 2159

12. Explain the significance of the number 144,000. Revelation 14:1, CCC 1138

* Discuss the significance of the word "number" in the verse of the song: *"I want to be in that number, when the Saints go marching in."*

13. Explore one aspect of worship in heaven.

Psalm 33:3
Psalm 96:1
Psalm 98:1
Revelation 14:1–3

* Write the titles of your three favorite hymns of praise to the Lord.

14. How will the Church be perfect in glory?

Revelation 14:4
CCC 778

15. What special vocational call or charism is described here?

Revelation 14:4
CCC 1618

* How would you explain to someone the good of virginity for the kingdom?

16. What event is announced in Revelation 14:7?

Revelation 14:7	
CCC 678	
CCC 681–682	

17. Describe the warning in Revelation 14:8–11.

18. Compare the following verses:

Matthew 11:28–29	
2 Thessalonians 1:7	
Revelation 14:13	

19. How does the son of man come in Revelation 14:14?

20. Describe the activity in Revelation 14:15–20.

* What comfort and reassurance can you find in Revelation 14:12?

Chapter 19

Companions of the Lamb
Revelation 15–16

And they sing the song of Moses, the servant of God,
and the song of the Lamb, saying,
"Great and wonderful are your deeds,
O Lord God the Almighty!
Just and true are your ways,
O King of the ages!
Who shall not fear and glorify your name, O Lord?
For you alone are holy.
All nations shall come and worship you, for your judgments have been revealed."
Revelation 15:3–4

The victors sing of the Lamb (Revelation 15:1–8)—A third sign appears in heaven. *"Then I saw another sign in heaven, great and wonderful, seven angels with seven plagues, which are the last, for with them the wrath of God is ended"* (Revelation 15:1). Following these plagues will be the judgment of Babylon. Here the sea of glass is mixed with fire indicating God's imminent judgment. *"Great and wonderful are your deeds, O Lord God the Almighty! Just and true are your ways, O King of the ages! Who shall not fear and glorify your name, O Lord? For you alone are holy. All nations shall come and worship you, for your judgments have been revealed"* (Revelation 15:3–4).

This hymn of victory is a composition of four Old Testament passages:

"How great are your works, O LORD!" (Psalm 92:5)
"God of faithfulness … just and right is he." (Deuteronomy 32:4)
"Who would not fear you, O King of the nations?" (Jeremiah 10:7)
"All the nations you have made shall come and bow down before you,
    O Lord, and shall glorify your name" (Psalm 86:9).

After this chant, glorifying God in His faithfulness to His promises, Saint John sees *"the temple of the tent of witness in heaven"* (Revelation 15:5), a composite metaphor from Exodus 40:24, signifying the presence of God in heaven. Issuing from this presence are seven angels, dressed like the Son of Man, receiving seven vials filled with the wrath of the eternal God from one of the living beings. His glory is underlined by the smoke that fills the temple, preventing anyone from interfering with the present course of action. Forerunners of this scenario can be found in the Old Testament. *"Then the cloud covered the tent of meeting, and the glory of the LORD filled the tabernacle.*

And Moses was not able to enter the tent of meeting, because the cloud abode upon it, and the glory of the LORD filled the tabernacle" (Exodus 40:34–35). *"And when the priests came out of the holy place, a cloud filled the house of the LORD, so that the priests could not stand to minister because of the cloud; for the glory of the LORD filled the house of the LORD"* (1 Kings 8:10–11). *"The place shall be unknown until God gathers his people together again and shows his mercy. And then the Lord will disclose these things, and the glory of the Lord and the cloud will appear, as they were shown in the case of Moses, and as Solomon asked that the place should be specially consecrated"* (2 Maccabees 2:7–8). These Old Testament passages foreshadow the advent of the Messiah and the restoration of His kingdom in the people of God.

The seven bowls (Revelation 16:1–21) — This vision is almost a literary twin to the vision of the seven trumpets in Revelation 8. Here is a selection of parallel features:

1st bowl, Revelation 16:2—Evil sores and ulcers inflict evil men. (1st trumpet, Revelation 8:7—Vegetation is burnt.)
2nd bowl, Revelation 16:3—All life in the sea is destroyed. (2nd trumpet, Revelation 8:8—One third of life is destroyed.)
3rd bowl, Revelation 16:4—Fresh waters become blood. (3rd trumpet, Revelation 8:10—Fire falls on one third of the waters.)
4th bowl, Revelation 16:8–9—Mankind is scorched with fierce heat and fire. (4th trumpet, Revelation 8:12—One third of light is destroyed.)
5th bowl, Revelation 16:10—The evil kingdom is darkened. (5th trumpet, Revelation 9:1–12—Locusts sting; smoke darkens the air.)
6th bowl, Revelation 16:12—The Euphrates dried up. (6th trumpet, Revelation 9:14—Euphrates' angels set free.)
7th bowl, Revelation 16:17–21—Lightning, thunder, earthquakes. (7th trumpet, Revelation 11:19—Lightning, thunder, earthquakes.)

Comparing these two septenaries of scourges, undeniably connected, shows that the apocalyptic genre repeats images and ideas in order to make a strong point. What characterizes the series of bowls is the fact that it punishes the whole world and strives for the conversion of all unrepentant sinners.

The book of Revelation shows that angels protect the natural elements—water, wind, and fire (Revelation 7:1, 14:18, 16:5). *"And the Lord will utterly destroy the tongue of the sea of Egypt"* (Isaiah 11:15), prepares the reader for the drying up of the river Euphrates in Revelation 16:12. This doom for Babylon was foretold by Jeremiah: *"I will plead your cause and take vengeance for you. I will dry up her sea and make her fountain dry; and Babylon shall become a heap of ruins"* (Jeremiah 51:36–37). The Euphrates River is the boundary of the Parthian kingdom, kings from the east, the epitome of danger and menace.

The image of the bowls of God's wrath seems to explain how God uses this ferocious people as an instrument to further His own plans, that is, to punish Rome. In other words, a world and its earthly powers without God propels itself toward doom and mutual self-destruction. Moreover, the *"foul demonic spirits like frogs"* (Revelation 16:13) are derived from the Mosaic plague in Egypt in Exodus 8:1–15. The ancient Hebrews considered the frog unclean (Leviticus 11:10). Three agents represent these foul or demonic spirits, the dragon, the beast, and the false prophet. The three representatives of evil form a satanic travesty, a triad in exact opposition to the beauty and grandeur of the Holy Trinity. Their mission is to convoke the evil kings on earth for the final battle against the Lamb and His heavenly armies (Revelation 19:11–21).

Saint Primasius († 560 AD), Bishop of Hadrumetum and Primate of Byzacena in Africa, looked at the frogs as if they were the symbols of heretics. He said that even as frogs emit an annoying croaking, so also the teachers of error make a great noise by their damnable rantings. He also said that the beast's guides, if allowed, would rule over our five senses as though he were their king.

"Behold, I am coming like a thief! Blessed is he who is awake, keeping his garments that he may not go naked and be seen exposed!" (Revelation 16:15) provides an interruption that urges the Christian readers in Asia Minor—and us today—that it is paramount to keep vigilant and ready, because the Lord may return when we least expect it. The preparedness of believers comprises the third beatitude of the Apocalypse. The sacred author then resumes his vision, by disclosing the place of assembly of ungodly armies. *"And they assembled them at the place which is called in Hebrew Armageddon"* (Revelation 16:16). Armageddon may possibly refer to the plain of Megiddo, south of Mount Carmel, well known to apocalyptic tradition (see Judges 5:19, 2 Kings 23:29, Zechariah 12:11, 2 Chronicles 35:22).

"The seventh angel poured his bowl into the air, and a great voice came out of the temple, from the throne, saying, 'It is done!' And there were flashes of lightning, loud noises, peals of thunder, and a great earthquake such as had never been since men were on the earth, so great was that earthquake" (Revelation 16:17–18). Here is a characteristic portrayal of the fate of all adversaries of God in this world, typified by the cities of

Rome and Babylon. All who oppose God will ultimately be destroyed. Unparalleled is the circumstance that the seventh vial is poured into the air, perhaps stressing the universality of the cataclysm. And God personally declares the verdict, confirming what was said in Revelation 14:8: "It is done!" the future has been decided and Babylon will have to drink the wine-cup of God's fury. This cosmic tumult is truly supreme and final. *"For in those days there will be such tribulation as has not been from the beginning of the creation which God created until now, and never will be"* (Mark 13:19). It would certainly be futile to search for concrete historical events of upheaval that would fit these descriptions. Our visionary on Patmos has recourse to these metaphors precisely to highlight the utter demolition of all those who prove to be opponents of God, inimical to the Lamb and unrepentant to the end.

Plagues of Egypt	**Trumpets**	**Bowls of Wrath**
Boils Exodus 9:9	Hail, fire, blood Revelation 8:7	Foul and evil sores Revelation 16:2
Nile is blood Exodus 7:20	Third of sea becomes blood Revelation 8:9	Sea became blood Revelation 16:3
Foul water–fish die Exodus 7:21	Men die of bitter water Revelation 8:10–11	Blood to drink Revelation 16:6
Darkness Exodus 10:22	Light was darkened Revelation 8:12	Kingdom in darkness Revelation 16:10
Locusts Exodus 10:13–15	Locusts torment men Revelation 9:3–10	Men scorched with fire Revelation 16:8
Frogs Exodus 8:6	Horses with lion's head Revelation 9:13ff	Foul spirits like frogs Revelation 16:13
Thunder and hail Exodus 9:23	Thunder and earthquake Revelation 10:3; 11:13	Lightning, thunder and a great earthquake Revelation 16:18

1. What does Saint John see in Revelation 15:1–3?

2. Compare the following songs of praise:

Exodus 15:1–2
Psalm 86:9–10
Psalm 145:17–20
Jeremiah 10:6–7
Revelation 15:3–4

* Write a song of praise to the Lord for the wonderful things He has done for you.

3. How were the angels dressed? Revelation 15:6

* How do you dress when you come before the Lord (at Mass)?

4. What physical property appears in the following passages?

Exodus 19:18
Song of Songs 3:6
Isaiah 6:4
Revelation 15:8

5. Describe another physical property that manifests the glory of the Lord.

1 Kings 8:10
Isaiah 4:5
Revelation 15:8
CCC 697

6. What physical thing does the Church use to show honor to God? Luke 1:8–10

* What physical things do Catholics routinely do to honor God?

7. What happens in the following verses?

Psalms 69:24	
Isaiah 66:6	
Revelation 16:1	

8. Explain the characteristic of God found in the following verses.

Deuteronomy 32:35	
Romans 12:19	
Hebrews 10:30–32	
Revelation 16:1	

* Define vengeance or "God's wrath" in your own words.

9. What kind of a judge is God? Revelation 16:5

Psalm 145:17	
John 5:26–30	
Revelation 16:5, 7	

10. What did the seven angels pour out from their bowls?

1st Angel   Revelation 16:2
2nd Angel   Revelation 16:3
3rd Angel   Revelation 16:4
4th Angel   Revelation 16:8
5th Angel   Revelation 16:10
6th Angel   Revelation 16:12ff
7th Angel   Revelation 16:17ff

11. How did the people respond to the torments of God's wrath? Revelation 16:9b

* Has there been a time in your life when you were stubborn, refusing to repent?

12. Why should a person repent?

Psalm 7:12
Sirach 17:24
Mark 1:14–15
Acts 2:38
Acts 3:19

13. What two things did God want the people to do? Revelation 16:9b

14. What sacrament does the Church offer to facilitate this? CCC 1456

15. How often must a practicing Catholic go to Confession? CCC 1457

* When was the last time you went to Confession? When can you next go?

16. How did some of the people respond to their pain? Revelation 16:10–11

17. What came from the mouth of the beast? Revelation 16:13–14

18. How will the final battle come about?

Matthew 24:42–44
Revelation 16:15

* If you were to meet Christ tonight, would you be ready? How could you prepare?

19. Where will the final battle take place? Revelation 16:16

20. Describe the final earthquake. Revelation 16:17–21

Chapter 20
Babylon has Fallen
Revelation 17–18

Then I heard another voice from heaven saying,
"Come out of her, my people,
lest you take part in her sins, lest you share in her plagues;
for her sins are heaped high as heaven,
and God has remembered her iniquities."
Revelation 18:4–5

The harlot of Babylon (Revelation 17:1–6)—To call unfaithful cities and territories a whore or harlot is well-known prophetic imagery in the Old Testament. *"For a spirit of harlotry has led them astray, and they have left their God to play the harlot"* (Hosea 4:12). *"How lovesick is your heart, says the Lord GOD, seeing you did all these things, the deeds of a brazen harlot"* (Ezekiel 16:30). Israel's fornication was considered a violation of her betrothal to God. *"Come, I will show you the judgment of the great harlot who is seated upon many waters, with whom the kings of the earth have committed fornication"* (Revelation 17:1–2) refers to the evil Babylon. Jeremiah the Prophet foretold the fall of Babylon with similar imagery: *"For the LORD has both planned and done what he spoke concerning the inhabitants of Babylon. O you who dwell by many waters, rich in treasures, your end has come, the thread of your life is cut"* (Jeremiah 51:12–13).

"The waters that you saw, where the harlot is seated, are peoples and multitudes and nations and tongues … the beast will hate the harlot; they will make her desolate and naked, and devour her flesh and burn her up with fire, for God has put it into their hearts to carry out his purpose by being of one mind and giving over their royal power to the beast, until the words of God shall be fulfilled" (Revelation 17:15–17). The symbol of harlotry as evil is clarified here. John is now carried away into a desert, or wilderness, and he sees *"a woman sitting on a scarlet beast which was full of blasphemous names"* (Revelation 17:3).

As Roman law required of prostitutes, this woman has her name written on her forehead, *"Babylon the great, mother of harlots and of the earth's abominations"* (Revelation 17:5). Babylon had been the epitome of rebellion against God from the very beginning of salvation history, when the people of Babel tried to build a tower to the heavens (Genesis 11:1–9). The mystery refers to the existence of so much iniquity, suffering, and evil in the world. This city, Babel or Babylon, now symbolizes any historical earthly power that stands opposed to the Lord. As a sure indication that this city is in opposition to the will of God, *"she is drunk with blood of the saints and the blood of the martyrs of Jesus"* (Revelation 17:6). In the early Christian period, the Roman empire persecuted and martyred Christians.

Wisdom explains the beast (Revelation 17:7-18)—*"The beast that you saw was, and is not"* (Revelation 17:8), is an obvious distortion of the eternal God, *"'I am the Alpha and the Omega,' says the Lord God, who is and who was and who is to come, the Almighty"* (Revelation 1:8). Satan has no creative powers. He can't make anything new or original. All Satan can do is to try to distort or pervert the perfection that God has created. The beast represents any political power that revolts against the Lordship of Jesus Christ. By its very nature, evil is doomed to fade away after a relatively short lifespan. God will only tolerate evil for a specified period of time. *"He comes and must remain only a little while"* (Revelation 17:10), and *"they are to receive authority as kings for one hour, together with the beast"* (Revelation 17:12) indicates that the Prince of this world can only reign until Christ comes again in Glory. Christ is the Victor. Evil doesn't get the last word.

"This calls for a mind with wisdom: the seven heads are seven hills on which the woman is seated" (Revelation 17:9) provides the reader with a sapiential key, that is, the clue which comes from wisdom. The seven hills are a clear allusion to the city of Rome, which was built on seven hills. The seven kings are simply the summation of anti-religious power, which will not last. Every single nation against which Isaiah prophesied (Isaiah 13–35) has vanished, be it Babylon, Moab, or Egypt. So must, ultimately, all nations perish who arraign themselves against God or ignore the laws of God. *"They will make war on the Lamb, and the Lamb will conquer them, for he is Lord of lords and King of kings, and those with him are called and chosen and faithful"* (Revelation 17:14) leaves no doubt that the wicked have declared their intention to wage war against the Lamb of God. Christians will suffer in Rome and elsewhere on this earth, as forewarned. But, evil will not succeed, for the King of Kings and Lord of Lords has the ultimate victory in history.

Internal strife and hatred, however, brings about corruption of all evil alliance. *"They and the beast will hate the harlot; they will make her desolate and naked, and devour her flesh and burn her up with fire, for God has put it into their hearts to carry out his purpose by being of one mind and giving over their royal power to the beast, until the words of God shall be fulfilled"* (Revelation 17:16–17). Jesus prophesied this very situation. *"For nation will rise against nation, and kingdom against kingdom; there will be earthquakes in various places, there will be famines; this is but the beginning of sufferings"* (Mark 13:8). Yet infinitely beyond all these vicissitudes of world history, the One True God reigns supreme, directing all destinies in accordance with His plan.

"Fallen, fallen is Babylon the great" (Revelation 18:1-24)—The fall of an enemy of God is considered a cosmic event in the Apocalypse. In his superb Bible knowledge, the Apostle John draws on his familiarity with Old Testament texts to illustrate the fall of Babylon. *"And Babylon, the glory of kingdoms, the splendor and pride of the Chaldeans, will be like Sodom and Gomorrah when God overthrew them. It will never be inhabited or dwelt in for all generations"* (Isaiah 13:19–20). *"Fallen, fallen is Babylon; and all the images of her gods he has shattered to the ground"* (Isaiah 21:9). *"Therefore wild beasts shall dwell with hyenas in Babylon, and ostriches shall dwell in her; she shall be* *peopled no more for ever, nor inhabited for all generations"* (Jeremiah 50:39). Babylon exemplifies self-centered immorality, surplus wealth, consumerism, global commerce and greed. These are some of the sins and deviations shared by the world community throughout human history. *"Come out of her, my people, lest you take part in her sins, lest you share in her plagues; for her sins are heaped high as heaven, and God has remembered her iniquities"* (Revelation 18:4–5). The Lord's patience is wearing thin, but He continues to show mercy toward His people. At this point the remnant of God-fearing people is exhorted to flee the city, as they have been instructed to do in the past. *"Flee from the midst of Babylon, let every man save his life! ... Forsake her, and let us go each to his own country; for her judgment has reached up to heaven and has been lifted up even to the skies ... Go out of the midst of her, my people! Let every man save his life from the fierce anger of the LORD!"* (Jeremiah 51:6,9,45). Jesus issued the same warning: *"But when you see the desolating sacrilege set up where it ought not to be (let the reader understand), then let those who are in Judea flee to the mountains"* (Mark 13:14). Hard times are coming, but God warns His people to be prepared.

"Render to her as she herself has rendered, and repay her double for her deeds" (Revelation 18:6). Here, the notion of retribution is rooted in prophetic literature. *"Bring upon them the day of evil; destroy them with double destruction! ... For this is the vengeance of the LORD: take vengeance on her, do to her as she has done. Cut off from Babylon the sower, and the one who handles the sickle in time of harvest"* (Jeremiah 17:18; 50:15–16). Saint Augustine adds: "The prophetic command is to be understood spiritually; we are to flee this earthly city, setting out for God with the steps of faith."

"Alas! alas! You great city, you mighty city, Babylon! In one hour has your judgment come" (Revelation 18:9). The prophetic proclamation on the city's demise which is about to begin recalls the vision of Ezekiel. *"How you have vanished from the seas, O city renowned, that was mighty on the sea, you and your inhabitants, who imposed your terror on all the mainland! Now the isles tremble on the day of your fall"* (Ezekiel 26:17–18). Mundane luxury and treasures are recalled, awaiting their utter disintegration in a very short time. A voice then addresses the saints in heaven, cheering them on to joyous celebration. *"Rejoice over her, O heaven, O saints and apostles and prophets, for God has given judgment for you against her!"* (Revelation 18:20). The demise of Babylon with great violence was foretold in Jeremiah. *"Thus shall Babylon sink, to rise no more, because of the evil that I am bringing upon her"* (Jeremiah 51:64), shedding light on the definitive end of Babylon. God will triumph over all evil.

Music, songs and shouts of joy fall silent as was foretold. *"The mirth of the timbrels is stilled, the noise of the jubilant has ceased"* (Isaiah 24:8). *"And I will make to cease from the cities of Judah and from the streets of Jerusalem the voice of mirth and the voice of gladness, the voice of the bridegroom and the voice of the bride; for the land shall become a waste"* (Jeremiah 7:34). *"And I will stop the music of your songs, and the sound of your lyres shall be heard no more"* (Ezekiel 26:13). All of these prophecies predict absolute devastation. Everyone loves a wedding. The voice of the bridegroom and the voice of the bride bring joy and give hope for new life. Marriage gives the hope of children and the continuation of a family, a community, a society. When the voice of the bridegroom and the voice of the bride are no longer heard, it means there are no more marriages, no more families, no more hope for the future. Marriage and family life are essential to the continuation of life and society. When marriage dies, civilization as we know it dies.

"And in her was found the blood of prophets and of saints, and of all who have been slain on earth" (Revelation 18:24) commemorates the suffering of the saints and martyrs, constituting the fallen city's greatest guilt. Here is what Jeremiah had spoken long ago: *"Babylon must fall for the slain of Israel, as for Babylon have fallen the slain of all the earth"* (Jeremiah 51:49). God will not be mocked. The saints of God will suffer greatly, but God will have the final word. At the moment, suffering and injustice seem incomprehensible. Why do good people suffer? Why has the Church of God been persecuted over the centuries? When will God come and rescue His people? When will justice and mercy come?

> Before Christ's second coming the Church must pass through a final trial that will shake the faith of many believers. The persecution that accompanies her pilgrimage on earth will unveil the "mystery of iniquity" in the form of a religious deception offering men an apparent solution to their problems at the price of apostasy from the truth. The supreme religious deception is that of the Antichrist, a pseudo-messianism by which man glorifies himself in place of God and of his Messiah come in the flesh.
>
> *Catechism of the Catholic Church 675*

> From the title of his book—*Apocalypse, Revelation*—the words "apocalypse, apocalyptic" were introduced into our language and, although inaccurately, they call to mind the idea of an incumbent catastrophe. The Book should be understood against the backdrop of the dramatic experiences of the seven Churches of Asia, which had to face serious difficulties at the end of the first century—persecutions and also inner tensions—in their witness to Christ. John addresses them, showing acute pastoral sensitivity to the persecuted Christians, whom he exhorts to be steadfast in the faith and not to identify with the pagan world. His purpose is constituted once and for all by the revelation, starting with the death and Resurrection of Christ, of the meaning of human history.
>
> The first and fundamental vision of John, in fact, concerns the figure of the Lamb who is slain yet standing, and is placed before the throne on which God Himself is already seated … The other thing is that Jesus Himself, precisely because He died and was raised, henceforth fully shares in the kingship and saving power of the Father. This is the fundamental vision.

On this earth, Jesus, the Son of God, is a defenseless, wounded and dead Lamb. Yet He stands up straight, on His feet, before God's throne and shares in the divine power. He has the history of the world in his hands. Thus, the Seer wants to tell us: trust in Jesus; do not be afraid of the opposing powers, of persecution! The wounded and dead Lamb is victorious! Follow the Lamb Jesus, entrust yourselves to Jesus, take His path! Even if in this world He is only a Lamb who appears weak, it is He who triumphs!

The subject of one of the most important visions of the Book of Revelation is this Lamb in the act of opening a scroll, previously closed with seven seals that no one had been able to break open. John is even shown in tears, for he finds no one worthy of opening the scroll or reading it. History remains indecipherable, incomprehensible. No one can read it. Perhaps John's weeping before the mystery of a history so obscure expresses the Asian Churches' dismay at God's silence in the face of the persecutions to which they were exposed at that time. It is a dismay that can clearly mirror our consternation in the face of the serious difficulties, misunderstandings and hostility that the Church also suffers today in various parts of the world.

These are the trials that the Church does not of course deserve, just as Jesus Himself did not deserve His torture. However, they reveal both the wickedness of man, when he abandons himself to the promptings of evil, and also the superior ordering of events on God's part. Well then, only the sacrificed Lamb can open the sealed scroll and reveal its content, give meaning to this history that so often seems senseless. He alone can draw from it instructions and teachings for the life of Christians, to whom His victory over death brings the message and guarantee of victory that they too will undoubtedly obtain …

Also at the heart of the visions that the Book of Revelation unfolds are the deeply significant vision of the Woman bringing forth a male child and the complementary one of the dragon, already thrown down from Heaven but still very powerful. This Woman represents Mary the Mother of the Redeemer, but at the same time she also represents the whole Church, the People of God of all times, the Church which in all ages, with great suffering, brings forth Christ ever anew. And she is always threatened by the dragon's power. She appears defenseless and weak. But while she is threatened, persecuted by the dragon, she is also protected by God's comfort. And in the end this Woman wins. The dragon does not win.

This is the great prophecy of his Book that inspires confidence in us! The Woman who suffers in history, the Church which is persecuted, appears in the end as the radiant Bride, the figure of the New Jerusalem where there will be no more mourning or weeping, an image of the world transformed, of the new world whose light is God Himself, whose lamp is the Lamb.

> For this reason, although John's Book of Revelation is pervaded by continuous references to suffering, tribulation and tears—the dark face of history—it is likewise permeated by frequent songs of praise that symbolize, as it were, the luminous face of history … Here we face the typical Christian paradox, according to which suffering is never seen as the last word but rather, as a transition towards happiness; indeed, suffering itself is already mysteriously mingled with the joy that flows from hope.
>
> For this very reason, John, the Seer of Patmos, can close his Book with a final aspiration, trembling with fearful expectation. He invokes the definitive coming of the Lord: "Come, Lord Jesus!"
>
> (Pope Benedict XVI, *General Audience*, August 23, 2006)

1. Explain the drama in Revelation 17:1–6.

2. Contrast the Woman of Revelation 12 with the harlot of Revelation 17.

White – "clothed with the sun" Revelation 12:1	*Colors –* Revelation 17:4
Life giving – "brought forth a male child" Revelation 12:5	Revelation 17:6
Stands against the darkness – "moon under her feet" Revelation 12:1	Revelation 17:2–3
Protected by God – Revelation 12:6	Revelation 17:16–17
Number – "crown of twelve stars" Revelation 12:1	*Numbers –* Revelation 17:3, 7

3. How is the beast portrayed as the opposite of God?

Revelation 1:8
Revelation 17:8

* Discuss some ways in which good and evil are opposites in today's society.

4. Find some ways to describe the Lord.

Daniel 2:47
Romans 1:1–6
1 Timothy 6:14–16
1 Peter 1:3; 2:9
Revelation 17:14

* What titles do you prefer to use when you pray to God?

5. Who does the woman (harlot) of Revelation 17 represent? Revelation 17:18

6. Compare Babylon's fall in Jeremiah and Revelation.

Jeremiah 51:7	Revelation 18:3
Jeremiah 51:9	Revelation 18:5
Jeremiah 50:29	Revelation 18:6
Jeremiah 51:30	Revelation 18:8
Jeremiah 51:48	Revelation 18:20
Jeremiah 51:49	Revelation 18:24

7. How does God warn His people?

Isaiah 48:20
Jeremiah 50:8–9
Revelation 18:4

* Have you ever heeded a warning sent by God?

8. What happens to those who conspire with evil? Revelation 18:9–10

9. Revelation 18:12–13 has the longest list of merchandise in the Bible. How many?

10. The last of the list is the most shocking. Explain. Revelation 18:13b

11. What happened to the delicacies? Revelation 18:14

12. How do the merchants react? Revelation 18:15–19

* Did you ever really long for something, but regret it later after you got it?

13. How quickly did the fortunes reverse? Revelation 18:19b

14. Who rejoiced over the fall of Babylon? Revelation 18:20

15. How is Babylon thrown down? Revelation 18:21

16. What happens to music in Babylon? Revelation 18:22

17. Why are craftsmen important in a society? Revelation 18:22b

18. Who will provide light for us in the future? Revelation 18:23; 21:23

19. Why is the voice of bride and bridegroom essential? Revelation 18:23b

* Is there a threat to marriage in society today? What could be done to help?

20. What was the major sin of Babylon or any evil society? Revelation 18:24

Chapter 21

The Marriage of the Lamb
Revelation 19–20

"Hallelujah! For the Lord our God the Almighty reigns.
Let us rejoice and exult and give him the glory,
for the marriage of the Lamb has come,
and his Bride has made herself ready;"
Revelation 19:6–7

Rejoicing in heaven (Revelation 19:1–10)—After the fall of the forces of evil, heaven resonates with praise and exultation. *"Hallelujah"* in Hebrew means "let us praise God," the typical and familiar Judeo-Christian liturgical acclamation of praise and rejoicing. All of the hymns of Revelation (Revelation 4:11; 5:9–13; 7:9–17; 11:15–18; 12:10–12; 14:3, 7; 15:3–4) culminate in these verses, as finally the blood of His servants has been avenged. The saints rejoice because God has judged the world, and good triumphs over evil. *"Hallelujah! Salvation and glory and power belong to our God, for his judgments are true and just; he has judged the great harlot who corrupted the earth with her fornication, and he has avenged on her the blood of his servants"* (Revelation 19:1–2). The great multitude in heaven is then followed by the hymn of the elders and living creatures, *"Amen, Hallelujah! … Praise our God, all you his servants, you who fear him, small and great"* (Revelation 19:4–5). Now alternating, it is the great multitude again that musically testifies to God's victorious reign in fulfillment of His promises to His people.

The Marriage of the Lamb—One of the most beautiful biblical images emerges here—the marriage covenant. God's everlasting communion with His elect is portrayed as the bond between a bridegroom and his bride. Marital imagery is brought to its fullness in the Incarnation of the God-Man Jesus Christ. God's immense love is shown in that He gave His only begotten Son for the redemption of the world. Jesus sheds His Precious Blood for His Bride the Church. God's immense love for His people is revealed from the beginning of the Bible to the end. *"For the LORD has called you like a wife forsaken and grieved in spirit"* (Isaiah 54:6). *"And in that day, says the LORD, you will call me, 'My husband'"* (Hosea 2:16). *"I feel a divine jealousy for you, for I betrothed you to Christ to present you as a pure bride to her one husband"* (2 Corinthians 11:2). *"Husbands, love your wives, as Christ loved the Church and gave himself up for her … This is a great mystery, and I mean in reference to Christ and the church"* (Ephesians 5:25,32).

Therefore, the history of the Church is like a marriage feast. *"Jesus spoke to them in parables, saying, 'The kingdom of heaven may be compared to a king who gave a marriage feast for his son, and sent his servants to call those who were invited to the marriage feast'"* (Matthew 22:1–2). John the Baptist identified Jesus as the bridegroom of the Church. *"I am not the Christ, but I have been sent before him. He who has the bride is the bridegroom; the friend of the bridegroom, who stands and hears him, rejoices greatly at the bridegroom's voice; therefore this joy of mine is now full"* (John 3:28–29). The wedding day of the Lamb symbolizes the inauguration of God's reign. Jesus is the Lamb of God. The Lamb's bride is the Church. Marriage is one of the biblical metaphors used to describe the covenant relationship between God and His people. Hence, idolatry and apostasy are viewed as adultery and harlotry. The Church is now in a courtship before her wedding.

Notice also the stark contrast between the metaphor of the harlot and that of the bride in these chapters. Saint Paul presents the imagery of a pure bride, faithful to her one husband. This is the imagery of the Church, pure and undefiled, faithful to the one true God, free of idolatry or divided allegiance. *"Blessed are those who are invited to the marriage supper of the Lamb,"* (Revelation 19:9) reveals a fourth beatitude as we receive the invitation to the wedding banquet of the Lamb. Saint Bede tells us that this banquet will be nothing other than the refreshment of the heavenly vision. At the close of this vision the seer is so overwhelmed by the splendor of the revelation that the angel had to remind him to worship God alone.

The Rider on the white horse (Revelation 19:11–21)—At this point the stage is set for the long-anticipated final combat. The idea of God, like a warrior, annihilating His enemies has Old Testament roots (Ezekiel 38; Zechariah 12; Joel 3:1–3). In Wisdom the eternal Word comes down like a stern warrior to execute God's decrees upon men. *"While gentle silence enveloped all things, and night in its swift course was now half gone, your all-powerful word leaped from heaven, from the royal throne, into the midst of the land that was doomed, a stern warrior carrying the sharp sword of your authentic command, and stood and filled all things with death, and touched heaven while standing on earth"* (Wisdom 18:14–16).

Various aspects of the Messiah, already revealed, are now woven together in a grand vision. *"Then I saw heaven opened, and behold, a white horse! He who sat upon it is called Faithful and True, and in righteousness he judges and makes war"* (Revelation 19:11). This verse fuses two common titles of God in the name of the Rider—Faithful and True. *"Know therefore that the LORD your God is God, the <u>faithful</u> God who keeps covenant and merciful love with those who love him and keep his commandments, to a thousand generations"* (Deuteronomy 7:9). *"This God—his way is perfect; the promise of the LORD proves <u>true</u>; he is a shield for all those who take refuge in him"* (2 Samuel 22:31). This promise was especially important for the people of God to remember in times of persecution and trials. *"He shall not judge by what his eyes see, or decide by what his ears hear; but with righteousness he shall judge the poor"* (Isaiah 11:3–4). God is faithful and true. He will judge with right judgment. Justice will be served.

Since Christ is the real King, His crowns, or diadems are without number, in contrast to the dragon, who had seven diadems (Revelation 12:3) and the beast who had ten diadems (Revelation 13:1). Christ is the real King with many diadems, many crowns, and so the people of God, who belong to Him, triumphantly sing: "Crown Him with Many Crowns, the Lamb upon His Throne!"

Whenever a name is mentioned in the Sacred Scriptures, the name identifies the essence of a person. Here, however, no one knows the Rider's real name, except His Father. *"All things have been delivered to me by my Father; and no one knows the Son except the Father, and no one knows the Father except the Son and any one to whom the Son chooses to reveal him"* (Matthew 11:27). Jesus is commonly called the Word of God. *"In the beginning was the Word, and the Word was with God, and the Word was God"* (John 1:1). In his epistle, Saint John identifies the Christians as belonging to the Word of God, who dwells within them. *"I write to you, young men, because you are strong, and the word of God abides in you, and you have overcome the evil one"* (1 John 2:14). The title "Word of God" emphasizes His mission to communicate the Father's will and love to us.

Isaiah 63:1 describes glorious crimson garments to prefigure His *"robe dipped in blood"* (Revelation 19:13). The Lord returns, triumphantly after defeating and punishing His adversaries, similar to someone who has trodden the winepress. Tellingly, His armies, that is, all the angels and saints, impress by their uniformity as they resemble their divine General in their garments. *"And the armies of heaven, wearing fine linen, white and pure, followed him on white horses"* (Revelation 19:14). The angels will help to round up the faithful. *"And then he will send out the angels, and gather his elect from the four winds, from the ends of the earth to the ends of heaven"* (Mark 13:27). And the saints will assist the Lord in judgment. *"Do you not know that the saints will judge the world?"* (1 Corinthians 6:2).

The Word's only weapon is a sharp sword from His mouth, with which He strikes the nations. Isaiah prophesied thus: *"He shall strike the earth with the rod of his mouth, and with the breath of his lips he shall slay the wicked"* (Isaiah 11:4). Saint Paul reiterates this truth: *"And then the lawless one will be revealed, and the Lord Jesus will slay him with the breath of his mouth and destroy him by his appearing and his coming"* (2 Thessalonians 2:8). That His rule will be comparable to a scepter of iron has already been expressed in the Psalms: *"You shall break them with a rod of iron, and dash them in pieces like a potter's vessel"* (Psalm 2:9).

In addition to His unknown name and the given name, *the Word,* He also *"has a name inscribed, King of kings, and Lord of lords"* (Revelation 19:16). God is about to defeat all opposing forces, and the outcome is described with apocalyptic language, derived from Ezekiel 39:17–22. A grotesque feast, the antithesis of the Lamb's supper, brings together the beast, the false prophet, and those who worshipped the false image. They are invited to toast their own downfall. Once again, the evil imagery is exactly the opposite of the sacred imagery, a profound perversion of goodness. Although the actual combat is not visualized, its conquest is accomplished with the word only. All evildoers, headed by the beast and his minions, are consigned to eternal destruction by fire. *"And the beast was captured, and with it the false prophet who in its presence had worked the signs by which he deceived those who had received the mark of the beast and those who worshipped its image. These two were thrown alive into the lake of fire that burns with brimstone. And the rest were slain by the sword of him who sits upon the horse, the sword that issues from his mouth"* (Revelation 19:20–21).

A thousand years (Revelation 20:1–10)—Satan is the actual driving force behind the beast and his false prophets. Now he is irreversibly judged. *"On that day the* LORD *will punish the host of heaven, in heaven, and the kings of the earth, on the earth. They will be gathered together as prisoners in a pit"* (Isaiah 24:21–22). Isaiah foretells the binding the powers of evil and darkness and imprisoning them. *"And he seized the dragon, that ancient serpent, who is the Devil and Satan, and bound him for a thousand years"* (Revelation 20:2). Many commentators have misinterpreted the thousand years as a period of peace and prosperity between the foundation of the Church and Christ's Parousia. This erroneous doctrine, called "millenarianism," supposed that after a first resurrection of the body, the faithful would reign with Christ, who would come to rule on earth for literally a thousand years' reign. This error resulted from taking a literal, fundamental interpretation of a symbolic mystical vision, and has been rejected by the Catholic Church.

In actuality, however, this thousand years' period represents the history of the Church, a long but finite stretch of time. *"But do not ignore this one fact, beloved, that with the Lord one day is as a thousand years, and a thousand years as one day"* (2 Peter 3:8). *"For a thousand years in your sight are but as yesterday when it is past, or as a watch in the night"* (Psalm 90:4). Satan has effectively been bound, that is, vanquished, at the moment of the Lord's Death and Resurrection. Satan is in a state of definitive defeat. *"Now is the judgment of this world, now shall the ruler of the world be cast out"* (John 12:31). Yet, the devil is still around, and will continue to create havoc for God's people until right before the glorious return of the divine Judge on the boundary of world history. Satan is allowed to bring about the universal upheaval that is the partial subject of this Apocalypse.

Thus, the millennium (the thousand years) begins from the moment of the defeat of Satan—from the Incarnation with its consummation in Jesus' Death–Resurrection–Ascension, and ends with His Second Coming in Glory, His Parousia. Consequently, the glorious rising and reigning of the saints with Christ, *"who reigned with Christ a thousand years"* (Revelation 20:4) alludes to the Body of Christ of which we become members through baptism. Baptism is the first resurrection. *"Do you not know that all of us who have been baptized into Christ Jesus were baptized into his death? We were buried therefore with him by baptism into death, so that as Christ was raised from the dead by the glory of the Father, we too might walk in newness of life"* (Romans 6:3–4). *"For as the Father has life in himself, so he has granted the Son also to have life in himself, and has given him authority to execute judgment, because he is the Son of man. Do not marvel at this; for the hour is coming when all who are in the tombs will hear his voice and come forth, those who have done good, to the resurrection of life, and those who have done evil, to the resurrection of judgment"* (John 5:26–29).

All those who proved to be loyal in their testimony for Christ are then assigned a share in the messianic role of judging, that is, reigning as priests of God and of Christ, as foretold by Isaiah. *"You shall be called the priests of the LORD, men shall speak of you as the ministers of our God"* (Isaiah 61:6). Daniel 7:9 sheds light on the thrones. *"Then I saw thrones, and seated on them were those to whom judgment was committed"* (Revelation 20:4a). Jesus told His apostles, *"Truly, I say to you, in the new world, when the Son of man shall sit on his glorious throne, you who have followed me will also sit on twelve thrones, judging the twelve tribes of Israel"* (Matthew 19:28). Jesus foretells and explains the believers' function as judges. What is intended here is our supernatural, sacramental life hidden with Jesus in God. Those who are not members of the Mystical Body, are clearly compromised and not spiritually alive during the thousand years of Church history. The natural lives of unbelievers could be seen as a first death. The second death signifies eternal damnation—the ultimate separation from God. The second death has absolutely no power over the believers.

After the thousand years, Satan will be let out for a little while. The devil will make one last desperate attempt to deceive as many as possible and snatch them away from the Lamb. The names of Gog and Ma'gog, which we studied in Ezekiel 38, symbolize the final campaign of evil against Christ and against His beloved City, the Church. Psalm 78:68 sings of God's love for Jerusalem, the embodiment of His kingdom on earth. Satan has now been irrevocably overcome and thrust into the lake of fire, and the stage is set for the Last Judgment.

General resurrection and last judgment (Revelation 20:11–15)—God Himself has the last word. God alone is the Judge of all as they rise to stand before His throne. There will be no appeal against His sentence. Earth and sky flee from God's awe-inspiring presence. They have to make way for the new (Revelation 21:1; Romans 8:19ff). Eternal books, including the mysterious Book of Life, are opened according to biblical promises. A great truth is expressed here. *"And the dead were judged by what was written in the books, by what they had done"* (Revelation 20:12). All people will be judged by their deeds. Deeds matter. Finally, death is destroyed, reminiscent of what Saint Paul had foretold. *"The last enemy to be destroyed is death"* (1 Corinthians 15:26). Isaiah prophesied: *"He will swallow up death for ever, and the Lord GOD will wipe away tears from all faces"* (Isaiah 25:8). This final annihilation is likened to a lake of fire, the diametrical opposite of the God of Life!

We have reached here a juncture that enables us to look back and realize a crucial truth regarding the structure of the book of Revelation. Although there are various *repetitions* of eschatological scenarios describing one and the same reality, that of the ongoing conflict between Dragon and Lamb (Revelation 4–11, 13–20), the narrative is even more importantly marked by a *rectilinear and dynamic* movement—especially following Revelation 12—towards the final resolution of this epic dualism, precisely through the judgment of Babylon the worldly city, the decisive battle, Last Judgment, and, coming up, the descent of the heavenly city. Hence, universal history is conceived as a pilgrimage towards a final rest.

1. Identify the common elements in three visions in Revelation.

Revelation 4:10	Revelation 11:16	Revelation 19:4
Revelation 4:8	Revelation 11:17	Revelation 19:6
Revelation 4:5	Revelation 11:19	Revelation 19:6b

2. Write your favorite verse from each of the hymns of Revelation.

Revelation 4:8–11
Revelation 5:9–14
Revelation 7:9–17
Revelation 11:15–18
Revelation 12:10–12
Revelation 14:3–7
Revelation 15:3–4
Revelation 19:1–3 Revelation 19:6–8

3. Write your two favorite contemporary hymns of praise to God.

4. What kind of a judge is God? Describe His judgments. Revelation 19:2a

5. Who receives judgment in Revelation 19:2b?

6. What happens in the following verses?

Isaiah 34:10	
Revelation 19:3	

7. Who worships God in Revelation 19:4–7?

8. What celebration is announced in Revelation 19:7–9?

* Describe the most joyful wedding celebration you ever attended.

** What can you personally do to support fidelity in marriage and fidelity to God?

9. Explain the kingdom of heaven and the Bride of the Lamb. CCC 865

10. What anticipates the wedding feast of the Lamb? CCC 1329

* How often and how joyfully do you participate in this event?

11. Describe two ways of seeing marriage in Sacred Scripture.

CCC 1602	
CCC 1612	

12. Describe the rider on the white horse. Revelation 19:11–16

13. Find five names for God in Revelation 19:11–16.

14. What ultimately happens to the beast and the false prophet? Revelation 19:20

15. What did Jesus foretell would be the result for evildoers?

Matthew 13:40–42
Mark 9:47–48
Luke 17:26–30

16. What does the Catholic Church teach about hell?

CCC 1033
CCC 1034
CCC 1035
CCC 1036

* Does God want or predestine anyone to go to hell? CCC 1037

** What could you do to avoid hell and to help others to avoid damnation?

17. Explain the Church's teaching on the thousand years.

Revelation 20:1–6
CCC 676

18. Where will Satan end up? Revelation 20:7–10

* Where do we get the term "fire and brimstone" and is this real?

19. Who will ultimately judge?

2 Timothy 4:1
Hebrews 10:30–31
Revelation 20:11–15

20. How and by Whom will you be judged? Revelation 20:12–13

* What happens to those whose names are NOT written in the book of life? Revelation 20:15

Chapter 22

New Heaven and Earth
Revelation 21–22

"Behold, the dwelling of God is with men.
He will dwell with them, and they shall be his people,
and God himself will be with them;
he will wipe away every tear from their eyes,
and death shall be no more,
neither shall there be mourning nor crying nor pain any more,
for the former things have passed away."
Revelation 21:3–4

The new creation (Revelation 21:1–8)—The vision of the new creation and new Jerusalem (Revelation 21:1–22:5) represents the most grandiose mosaic in the choicest of biblical images, synthesizing them into a climactic icon of a luminous depiction of God's everlasting love for His sons and daughters. Indeed, Saint Paul has said, *"What no eye has seen, nor ear heard, nor the heart of man conceived, what God has prepared for those who love Him!"* (1 Corinthians 2:9). Saint John is speaking here as the unchallenged theologian of the *Eschaton* (time of consummation). Other scriptural passages depict the holy city: *"But the Jerusalem above is free, and she is our mother"* (Galatians 4:26), either as a community *"But you have come to Mount Zion and to the city of the living God, the heavenly Jerusalem, and to innumerable angels in festal gathering, and to the assembly of the first born who are enrolled in heaven"* (Hebrews 12:22–23), or as a city built in heaven. Consider the trajectory from the garden to Abraham's simple nomad tent (Genesis 12:8) to the highest form of civilization imaginable, the city of God!

"Then I saw a new heaven and a new earth; for the first heaven and the first earth had passed away, and the sea was no more" (Revelation 21:1). Ancient peoples feared the sea as a place of storms and shipwrecks. The sea could also be a place of danger and the abode of the dead, in the case of drowning. The reason for the destruction of the sea is that it was the traditional dwelling place of the primordial chaos and of the sea-monster (Genesis 1:21), the dragon. This abode of inveterate rebellion against God cannot possibly subsist in the new creation, it is totally incompatible with the presence of God's peace.

Isaiah foretells *"For behold, I create new heavens and a new earth; and the former things shall not be remembered or come into mind. But be glad and rejoice for ever in that which I create"* (Isaiah 65:17–18). He also predicts the city to be like a bride (Isaiah 61:10; 62:4ff). Now, in Revelation, these prophecies are being fulfilled. Notice the axis of conflicting symbols, which at the same time unify the narrative of Revelation: the cosmic woman (Revelation 12), the harlot of Babylon (Revelation 17), and now the bride, *"And I saw the holy city, new Jerusalem, coming down out of heaven from God, prepared as a bride adorned for her husband"* (Revelation 21:2).

"Behold, the dwelling of God is with men. He will dwell with them, and they shall be his people, and God himself will be with them; he will wipe away every tear from their eyes, and death shall be no more, neither shall there be mourning nor crying nor pain any more, for the former things have passed away" (Revelation 21:3–4). These verses highlight the ultimate accomplishment of the constant prophecies of a life-communion between God and man. *"And I will walk among you, and will be your God, and you shall be my people"* (Leviticus 26:12). *"I have loved you with an everlasting love; therefore I have continued my faithfulness to you … I will be their God, and they shall be my people"* (Jeremiah 31:3, 33). *"My dwelling place shall be with them; and I will be their God and they shall be my people"* (Ezekiel 37:27). His presence among us (Hebrew *shekina*) typifies the Covenant and the glory of God, *"Then the cloud covered the tent of meeting, and the glory of the LORD filled the tabernacle"* (Exodus 40:34). This culminates in the indissoluble marriage between God and man in Christ's Incarnation (called *hypostatic union*), *"The glory which you have given me I have given to them, that they may be one even as we are one"* (John 17:22).

Moreover, the era of unprecedented joy has been ushered in. *"Shout, and sing for joy, O inhabitant of Zion, for great in your midst is the Holy One of Israel"* (Isaiah 12:6). God has accomplished the victory over sin and death. *"The LORD your God is in your midst, a warrior who gives victory; he will rejoice over you with gladness, he will renew you in his love; he will exult over you with loud singing as on a day of festival"* (Zephaniah 3:17–18). Saint Paul explains the complete newness of it all. *"Therefore, if any one is in Christ, he is a new creation; the old has passed away, behold, the new has come"* (2 Corinthians 5:17).

Now, God speaks for the first time in Revelation. *"'Behold, I make all things new.' Also he said, 'Write this, for these words are trustworthy and true.' And he said to me, 'It is done! I am the Alpha and the Omega, the beginning and the end. To the thirsty I will give water without price from the fountain of the water of life. He who conquers shall have this heritage, and I will be his God and he shall be my son. But as for the cowardly, the faithless, the polluted, as for murderers, fornicators, sorcerers, idolaters, and all liars, their lot shall be in the lake that burns with fire and brimstone, which is the second death'"* (Revelation 21:5–8). Christian readers of the message, the conquerors, are profoundly reassured concerning God's providence as the trustworthy Alpha and Omega, the Truth from beginning to end.

The fountain of the water of life, recalls earlier prophecies. Isaiah foretold: *"With joy you will draw water from the wells of salvation"* (Isaiah 12:3) and *"For I will pour water on the thirsty land, and streams on the dry ground; I will pour my Spirit upon your descendants and my blessing on your offspring"* (Isaiah 44:3). Ezekiel envisioned water flowing from the temple (Ezekiel 47:1). Water is essential for life in any culture or time. And water in the New Testament often symbolizes the divine Spirit. Jesus explained, *"Whoever drinks of the water that I shall give him will never thirst; the water that I shall give him will become in him a spring of water welling up to eternal life"* (John 4:14). And later, Jesus said, *"He who believes in me, as the Scripture has said, 'Out of his heart shall flow rivers of living water.' Now this he said about the Spirit, which those who believed in him were to receive"* (John 7:38–39).

One should pay close attention to the correlation between the promises attached to the letters to the suffering churches at the beginning of Revelation, and the fulfillment of those promises in this dazzling vision. God made a marvelous promise to Nathan about David in the Old Testament. *"I will be his father, an he shall be my son. When he commits iniquity, I will chasten him with the rod of men, with the stripes of the sons of men; but I will not take my merciful love from him"* (2 Samuel 7:14–15). Jesus, the anointed King, fulfills this promise in His Resurrection into which all His faithful are drawn. *"And we bring you the good news that what God promised to the fathers, this he has fulfilled to us their children by raising Jesus"* (Acts 13:32–33).

Lastly, the vice catalogue *"murderers, fornicators, sorcerers, idolaters, and all liars"* (Revelation 21:8) reflects earlier biblical lists of serious sins that will exclude people from enjoying the riches of the kingdom of God. *"They were filled with all manner of wickedness, evil, covetousness, malice. Full of envy, murder, strife, deceit, malignity, they are gossips, slanderers, haters of God, insolent, haughty, boastful, inventors of evil, disobedient to parents, foolish, faithless, heartless, ruthless. Though they know God's decree that those who do such things deserve to die, they not only do them but approve those who practice them"* (Romans 1:29–32). Saint Paul repeatedly warned people about the dangers of unrepentant sin, and encouraged them to turn to God. *"Let us then cast off the works of darkness and put on the armor of light; let us conduct ourselves becomingly as in the day, not in reveling and drunkenness, not in debauchery and licentiousness, not in quarreling and jealousy. But put on the Lord Jesus Christ, and make no provision for the flesh, to gratify its desires"* (Romans 13:12–14).

The new Jerusalem (Revelation 21:9–22:5)—An existence of surpassing bliss and beauty awaits those who have persevered in their trials here on earth and remained faithful to God. *"And in the Spirit he carried me away to a great, high mountain, and showed me the holy city Jerusalem coming down out of heaven from God"* (Revelation 21:10). The apostle's prototype for the portrayal of these heavenly realities was seen in Ezekiel 40–48. Both the twelve patriarchs and the twelve apostles, inscribed on gates and foundations, are reminding the city-dwellers of the historical roots of their beatitude. The city's measurements are taken, no longer for its protection but rather in exploration of its harmonious stability. Its effulgence is highlighted by the enormity of its dimensions and the radiance of its building materials, prefigured in Isaiah, *"I will set your stones in antimony, and lay your foundations with sapphires"* (Isaiah 54:11). Everything breathes grandeur, majesty, and unfading brilliance. The precious stones of jasper, sapphire, agate, emerald, onyx, carnelian, chrysolite, beryl, topaz, chrysoprase, jacinth, and amethysts generally correspond to the stones chosen for the high priest's breastplate of judgment (Exodus 28:17; 39:10).

Isaiah prophesied, *"Arise, shine; for your light has come, and the glory of the LORD has risen upon you ... The sun shall no longer be your light by day, nor for brightness shall the moon give light to you by night; but the LORD will be your everlasting light, and your God will be your glory"* (Isaiah 60:1, 19). Isaiah's prophecy is fulfilled here. *"And I saw no temple in the city, for its temple is the Lord God the Almighty and the Lamb. And the city has no need of sun or moon to shine upon it, for the glory of God is its light, and its lamp is the Lamb"* (Revelation 21:22–23). This illustrates God's accomplishment of rapturous peace as He promised. God is no longer hidden in a temple, now He is the infinite light for all to see in the absence of any form of darkness. *"God is light and in him is no darkness at all"* (1 John 1:5). The city has forever transcended the dichotomy between light and darkness, good and evil, the sacred and the profane. The divine now transforms everything; everything has become a translucent Tabor.

Yet another layer of symbolism is added on to this supernatural oil on canvas. The new city is also compared to a garden with a river, fruit trees, and the tree of life in Revelation 22:1–2. The history of humanity started in a garden in Eden, with a river, fruit trees and a tree of life (Genesis 2:9–3:22). The reader is taken back to the state of affairs before Adam and Eve fell and brought sin into the world. The unfathomable logic and graciousness of God's designs are stunning. After having been expelled from that first paradise, humanity has come home at last to a new paradise. First and last things (*protology* and *eschatology*) truly come full circle. People's utopian hopes and dreams finally coincide with God's plan! Gushing river, verdant tree and lush fruits illustrate the plenitude of enjoyment of life.

"His servants shall worship him; they shall see his face" (Revelation 22:3–4), signals the vertiginous summit of biblical spirituality—to see God, face to face, and live! This is a privilege not granted to us mortals in this present life. Moses asked to see God, but God told Moses, *"You cannot see my face; for man shall not see me and live"* (Exodus 33:20). Jesus promised that one day we could see God. *"Blessed are the pure in heart, for they shall see God"* (Matthew 5:8). God made Himself known to humanity through Jesus. *"No one has ever seen God; the only-begotten Son, who is in the bosom of the Father, he has made him known"* (John 1:18). Saint Paul explains, *"For now we see in a mirror dimly, but then face to face"* (1 Corinthians 13:12). We are further exhorted to *"Strive for peace with all men, and for the holiness without which no one will see the Lord"* (Hebrews 12:14). In a previous letter, Saint John wrote, *"Beloved, we are God's children now; it does not yet appear what we shall be, but we know that when he appears we shall be like him, for we shall see him as he is"* (1 John 3:2). This glorious vision climaxes in total and unutterable happiness. What an amazing utopia toward which our dark, dire, and disconcerting history is headed!

Amen, Come Lord Jesus (Revelation 22:6–21)—In this closing section of the Apocalypse, the dramatization of three voices reaffirm the purpose of this writing. The three persons speaking are Jesus, an angel, and John, although it is not always clear where one stops speaking and the other begins. *"These words are trustworthy and true"* (Revelation 22:6) assure the reader that this message is credible, reaffirming what the angel said in

Revelation 19:9, and God spoke in the previous chapter (Revelation 21:5). Saint John is reckoned among the prophets in the fifth beatitude of this book, *"Blessed is he who keeps the words of the prophecy of this book"* (Revelation 22: 7b).

Then John is again overcome by the impact of these visions, and falls down to worship at the feet of the angel. The angel admonishes John that he is a fellow servant, and worship belongs to God alone. Suddenly the angel is no longer speaking, but Jesus begins, *"Behold, I am coming soon, bringing my recompense, to repay every one for what he has done. I am the Alpha and the Omega, the first and the last, the beginning and the end"* (Revelation 22:12–13). The voice of Christ proclaims the imminence of His return as Judge. He will requite everyone according to his works. *"For the Son of Man is to come with his angels in the glory of his Father, and then he will repay every man for what he has done"* (Matthew 16:27).

There is a sixth beatitude, *"Blessed are those who wash their robes that they may have the right to the tree of life and that they may enter the city by the gates"* (Revelation 22:14). Each person must be cleansed and made ready to approach the tree of life. Jesus Himself pledges for the authenticity of this testimony to the Church. *"I Jesus have sent my angel to you with this testimony for the churches. I am the root and the offspring of David, the bright morning star"* (Revelation 22: 16). The Church longs for Jesus to return in glory to inaugurate the city of light: *"The Spirit and the Bride say, 'Come.'"* (Revelation 22:17). A stern warning is given to anyone who tries to distort or alter the contents of this prophecy. Revelation concludes with a liturgical request: *"Come, Lord Jesus!"* (*Maranatha!*)

Revelation is the definitive seal on Matthew 16:18: *"I tell you, you are Peter, and on this rock I will build my church, and the powers of death shall not prevail against it."* John's worldview is firmly dualistic: there is God and there is evil. The dualism is relative, however, and not absolute, as God remains in control at all times, until the ultimate victory of good over evil. He clearly perceives the threat to Christians that is constituted by a worldly authority under the dominion of evil, identified with the beast. John encourages Christians to persevere, not conjuring up false hopes of miraculous intervention but by trusting and understanding the value of their sufferings. Perseverance and patience are the virtues practiced amid trials and tribulations. The enduring comfort is that the powerless victims, suffering for Christ, would be the ultimate victors. Believers today need not worry about sufferings and hardships. Whatever beasts, demons, dragons, harlots, antichrists, persecutions or sufferings a Christian might encounter in this life, Jesus assures us that He will be with us through it all. And there will be a new heaven and a new Jerusalem awaiting the just for all eternity.

1. What can you learn about awaiting the new Jerusalem?

Romans 8:19–23
2 Peter 3:11–13
Revelation 21:1–4
CCC 756
CCC 757
CCC 2016

2. Explain a Marian perspective on the dwelling of God and ark of the Covenant.

Revelation 21:3
CCC 2676

3. When and how will this revelation be fulfilled?

Revelation 21:4
CCC 1044
CCC 1045

4. Explain the anagogical sense of Scripture in Revelation 21–22. CCC 117.3

5. Who speaks to John? What can you learn about Him?

Revelation 1:8
Revelation 21:5–6

6. Compare the following verses:

Psalm 89:26–28
Revelation 21:7

7. What kinds of people are listed in Revelation 21:8? What is their end lot?

8. Who is described in Revelation 21:9–14? CCC 865

9. Describe the new Jerusalem. Revelation 21:10–25

10. Compare the visions in Isaiah and Revelation.

Isaiah 60:19	Revelation 21:23
Isaiah 60:3–5	Revelation 21:24
Isaiah 60:11	Revelation 21:25–26

11. Explain the source of light.

John 8:12
Revelation 21:23
Revelation 22:5

12. Describe the vision in Revelation 22:1–5.

* How do you envision heaven?

13. What can you find in Genesis 2:9 and Revelation 22:2?

14. For what do we ultimately hope?

Revelation 22:4
CCC 1023
CCC 1029

15. Compare some passages at the beginning of Revelation to some at the end.

Revelation 1:1	Revelation 22:6
Revelation 1:3a	Revelation 22:7
Revelation 1:3b	Revelation 22:10

16. What is promised in Revelation 22:12–13?

17. How can you get the right to enter the city? Revelation 22:14–15, CCC 1470

* How often should you avail yourself of this opportunity for grace?

18. Explain Revelation 22:17.

Revelation 22:17
CCC 1130
CCC 2550

19. What warning is issued in Revelation 22:18–19?

20. When, where and why do we say, "Come, Lord Jesus!"

Revelation 22:20
CCC 524
CCC 671
CCC 796

* How does the Bible end? Do you find this hopeful or helpful? Explain